Coaching Winning
SOCCER

Coaching Winning
SOCCER

Willy Roy
and
Jim Walker

Contemporary Books, Inc.
Chicago

Library of Congress Cataloging in Publication Data

Roy, Willy.
    Coaching winning soccer.

    1.   Soccer coaching.   I. Walker, Jim.   II. Title.
GV943.8.R69 1979   796.33′4′077   78-73680
ISBN 0-8092-7458-2
ISBN 0-8092-7457-4 pbk.

Published by Contemporary Books, Inc.
180 North Michigan Avenue, Chicago, Illinois 60601
Manufactured in the United States of America
Library of Congress Catalog Card Number: 78-73680
International Standard Book Number: 0-8092-7458-2 (cloth)
                                        0-8092-7457-4 (paper)

Published simultaneously in Canada by
Beaverbooks
953 Dillingham Road
Pickering, Ontario L1W 1Z7
Canada

FOR LEE STERN
who put his money where his mouth is
for soccer

Contents

Acknowledgments

To Karen, Willy, Jr., Karsten, and Marc for their support; to Shirley, Kelly, and Danny for their patience; to Basil Kane for his expertise; to Bill Smith for his photos; to Dick Hoover for his advice; to Marcia Hardrick for her typing.

Introduction

The idea for this book was hatched on the eve of the 1978 North American Soccer League season when a friend who is a literary agent called and said he wanted a book on soccer.

On coaching soccer. On coaching *winning* soccer.

I knew right away he had heard about my masterful coaching of the Deerfield Booters, a lollipop brigade of ten-year-olds in the Young Sportsmens' Soccer League.

As a matter of fact, he said, he had not known about my coaching exploits, but figured I could put together an interesting textbook for coaches because the Sting was a team destined for glory.

"You're the General Manager, right?" he said.

"I'm generally managing," I replied.

"Well, you and the coach ought to be able to produce quite a book on coaching."

I agreed, and the contract was signed for a future great work of art.

The Sting lost its first game. I decided to delay the start of the first draft. The Sting lost its second game and I said, a bit uncomfortably, "Wait until we win one."

By this time, my boss, Clive Toye, the Sting's president and the man responsible for bringing the great Pele to the United States, had gotten wind of the book. He asked, a bit peevishly, because he perhaps thought I could be putting my time to better use with the team struggling so: "Well, when are you going to start?"

"This week," I replied meekly. "Soon as we start winning."

But defeat reared his ugly head again and the losses continued, one atop the next, careening toward record-setting proportions.

"How in the bloody hell," roared Toye, his

WILLY ROY, a winning coach.

beard bristling, "are *you* going to write a book about winning soccer?"

Red-faced, I didn't reply.

To the literary agent the next day, I roared, "How in the bloody hell am I going to write a book about winning soccer?

"Write," said the agent. "The book won't be published until the season's over and you'll have a winner."

I admired the agent's confidence in the book's future, but despaired over prospects for the team.

Toye apparently was despairing over the future of my book, so he provided the inspiration that so many writers wait so long for.

He changed coaches.

Enter inspiration. Enter Willy Roy. Enter Winning Soccer.

With Willy freshly minted as the new coach, the Sting caught fire to finish the season in the blaze of glory expected earlier, winning ten of the last 14 games to reach the North American Soccer League playoffs.

What magic did Roy bring to the team that caused the turnabout?

No magic, according to Dick Advocaat, a feisty little midfielder who suffered silently through the victory drought and became one of the key performers when the team started to win.

"The most important thing for a coach is how he treats his players," said Advocaat. "I'm a professional, and I know the techniques of playing. It's the same with the other players. What Willy did was stimulate us. He got us to play the game the way he wants it played.

"He knows us as a team and as individuals. And we know exactly what he expects from us. Have you ever heard him at halftime when we're playing poorly? It's a good thing if you haven't, because it isn't very pleasant for your ears.

"That's only when we're playing poorly. If we're losing at halftime and playing well, he will encourage us and pat us on the back. He knows a lot about people and how they feel. He also knows a lot about soccer."

And a lot about winning.

Success and Willy Roy were not strangers. His first taste of victory came as a high school wrestler when he won the state championship at the 145-pound level. He later earned All-Big Ten and All-American honors at the University of Illinois in the 167-pound category.

With his wrestling days behind him, Willy turned all his attention to his true sports love, soccer. In 1967, he was drafted by the Chicago Spurs and wound up as the league's Rookie of the Year, finishing second among the loop's scorers with 17 goals. Before his playing career ended, he had scored 42 goals and assisted on 29 others to rank him among the North American Soccer League's all-time scorers.

Meanwhile, he appeared 38 times for the United States National Team and earned 22 full caps, more than any American player in history.

Are you beginning to get the idea? Willy Roy is a winner. He was first in line when they passed out positive thinking and he's acquired the knack of passing it on to others and making winners of them, too.

Willy and I have set out to present an orderly discussion of how to coach winning soccer, at once within the range of beginners and still

Picking the team.

A word of encouragement.

Ready for the kickoff.

beneficial to all youth levels and other non-professional students of coaching.

The parent or other man or woman bitten by the coaching bug may be involved in many uncomfortable situations before learning to "ring the bell" and consistently turn in a performance of which he or she can be proud. He is not permitted to forget that he is a beginner, an apprentice, who must learn by trial and error. He will send his team against opponents directed by more experienced and more skilled coaches. He must not be thin-skinned about losses and must expect to receive criticism and advice. He must learn to file away in his mental scrapbook those pieces of wisdom that fit into his philosophy and discard those well-meaning suggestions that are contrary to his own objectives.

Of course, a former player begins with a built-in head start—knowledge of the game and a feeling for the successes and failures that occur in the game. But, even with that experience, he finds coaching a different ball game because he must concern himself not only with his own performance but the activities of all his players.

Whatever your background, it's your future we're interested in . . . as a winning coach.

—Jim Walker

1

No Time for Losing: What It Takes to Be a Winning Coach

To come right out with it, this is a book on winning.

There are many books about coaching soccer. Most provide guidelines for the teaching of fundamentals, playing for the game's sake, building character and having milkshakes after the game. There isn't, of course, anything wrong with all this, as far as it goes.

There is nothing wrong in wanting to win, either. That is the reward we seek whenever we play games. Whatever other intrinsic values you are able to learn or teach along the way should become a springboard to success.

There is no time for losing. The someone who said, "Show me a good loser and I'll show you a *real* loser," hit the nail on the head.

Winning begins with you, the coach. You must believe in yourself as a winner. If your purpose is not to win, then it leaves only one alternative—losing. There is not likely to be a book titled *Coaching Losing Soccer* or *The Technique of Losing*. Losers go home in the dark and fade into obscurity. Winners go on to bigger and better things.

As a coach, you must never teach your players how to beat the rules, but how to beat the opponent. There is no room for the coach who permits breaking the rules to achieve an advantage.

But all good coaches instill in their players a burning desire to win—win every ball, win every game.

Imparting that pride in winning to your players is a big job . . . but it *is* your job.

If there is one sport where pride can make the difference between winning and losing, it is soccer. Put two teams with comparable ability on the field and chances are it will be pride more than systems or tactics that will prevail. Systems and tactics are important, and you

Cosmos' Werner Roth grasps prized possession—North American Soccer League championship trophy—as 76,000 fans cheer.

must learn to match these effectively with your players' skills. But without pride, without a steadfastness in purpose, a team will taste defeat, whether it's a squad of ten-year-olds or professionals.

Call it positive thinking, if you like. But positive thinking can run to two extremes.

There was the ten-year-old center forward who said to his coach before a game: "Sir, those boys are bigger than we are and I think we're going to lose."

"Now that's not the right attitude," the coach admonished, "You must think positively."

"Okay," the little fellow said sadly, "I'm positive we're going to lose."

Better, follow the lead of one of the authors when asked in an interview, "Barring the unforeseen, will your team win this week?"

"What do you mean?" came the reply, "There isn't going to be any unforeseen!"

Believe in yourself as a coach who can and will teach soccer players something vital—to play better and to win.

Today is the beginning of the rest of your life . . . and your coaching career. Move forward, now, toward more confidence in yourself, increased knowledge of the game, a better understanding of people and what makes them tick and fulfillment of your own unique potential to manage players of soccer.

Know thyself. Then learn all you can about your players. Before converting your own winning philosophy into a winning team effort, you must know a few things about those human beings, whatever the age, who will look to you for guidance.

CHARACTER

Find out what your players are made of. Which ones have been babied, which of them are fighters, who among them will sacrifice for the good of the team?

You must deal on an individual level before you can generate an effective winning team attitude. Sometimes this is merely taking an interest in each player. Ask him how he feels, whether he's had a good day in school or at work, or how things are going at home. Even at the professional level, players like to know their coach is interested in them as people as well as players.

On a given day, you might permit a player to take it easy during a training session. Tell him you realize he's had a tough day and don't get on his case. Let him, on that day, set his own pace. If that player has character, he will appreciate your concern and come back the next day giving you an effort even he didn't know he possessed. If he lacks character, he'll try to take advantage of you and dog it another day. That's when you have to nip it in the bud and make him do what he doesn't want to do.

There have been countless players who have tried and failed to make it to the professional level simply because they were able to handle the easy parts of soccer, but had not conditioned themselves to withstand the hard work necessary to overcome setbacks along the way.

Elements of character sometimes don't fully reveal themselves until the crucial minutes of a game. That is when the player with character will push himself through the pain barrier, that excruciating time when the legs are heavy with fatigue and the body wracked with distress. He will want the ball at his feet then, while others will think, "Please don't pass the ball to me . . . let someone else screw this up."

Knowing which players will rise to these occasions can make a difference between victory and defeat.

REACTION TO CRITICISM

"It really makes me mad the way the coach yells at me," exclaimed the red-faced high school winger.

"Yeah? Well, I get even more teed off," replied his teammate.

"What do you mean?"

"He doesn't yell at me at all."

Which of your players will respond to constructive castigation? Which of them need individual counseling? Who needs a verbal kick in the pants, who requires a pat on the back?

Some players thrive on being corrected in front of their teammates. They will put forth extra effort to avoid the same mistake again. Others will be demoralized and, in their confusion, commit further mistakes. Those players need to be drawn into post-practice discussions about their performance.

It is important that you convert criticism into praise at the proper time.

During a scrimmage, a young professional defender failed to mark his man tightly enough, was beaten and a goal resulted. His coach pointed out the error and accused the defender of failing to hustle. The player turned on his coach with a look of defiance, and spat out some ill-chosen words. Angered, the coach ordered him to the sidelines and replaced him. After a time, the coach stopped the scrimmage, sent the erring defender back onto the field at the same position, and instructed the opposing side to play the ball at him. In rapid succession, the defender wrecked one attacking foray with a sliding tackle, headed away a dangerous cross and snuffed out another drive with a clean interception.

The coach praised him openly and the defender was a new man.

INTER-RELATIONSHIPS

Study your players' reactions to each other. Do certain players work better together than others? This may influence your team alignment. A center-forward who won't pass the ball to his left wing because he feels he won't get it back may hold onto the ball too long, force bad passes away from the left side or develop a habit of always passing to his right wing, thus setting up a tendency for an opponent to defense.

Build a happy team. Break the monotony of training sessions and games by getting your players together socially, maybe for a cookout or a party.

There was no open dissension, but neither was there much overall friendship, when the Chicago Sting was suffering through a record-setting string of losses at the beginning of the 1978 season. Nor was much effort made to bring the team closer togther.

When a coaching change was made, the new coach pointed this out at his first team meeting. "We're going to be friends," he said, "and we're going to be doing things together."

There were more team meals and, after the victories became more frequent, post-game parties. Occasionally, there would be a team visit to tourist attractions on road trips. There was more player participation in team meetings. Players found themselves liking teammates that previously they had barely spoken to off the field. The change revealed itself on the field almost immediately. The players were pulling for each other, praising one another and playing as a team.

The Sting rejected its losing ways for a glorious finish that may have saved the franchise from moving out of Chicago.

SKILL FACTOR

The skills of your players are very important, obviously, but only important in the context of the team. Learn to use the skills of your players to build team performance.

Don't seek the impossible. Give players responsibilities for which they have the aptitude and they will excel.

A center-forward who is weak on heading the ball won't perform well if his teammates consistently give him balls in the air. Speak to his teammates and discuss frankly his weaknesses and strong points.

"Let's face it," you might confide to a midfielder, "Joe doesn't take high balls well. But he's very effective when he can collect the ball on the ground. Let's feed them to his feet."

Make your players think they're smarter as a team than the opponent.

"Our opponent has more stars," you tell your squad, "but we're better as a team. We're better than *any* team with individual stars."

They will respond.

ATTITUDE

Once you have determined the character of your players, their reaction to criticism, interrelationships and skill factor, it all comes down to attitude, yours and theirs.

Good attitudes toward each other, toward you as a coach and toward practicing will determine whatever success your team attains.

Willingness to push themselves to prove individual skills and maintain a high level of teamwork is a manifestation of good player attitude.

The player who wants to pack it in ten minutes before practice is over will often be the same player who gives up in a game with your team down a goal and ten minutes to play.

Good coaching attitude is just as important. Show confidence, but never be fully satisfied with your team's performance. Soccer is a game of mistakes and you should prepare your team in such a way that it will make fewer than its opponents. It seems a tired old saw, but take each game as it comes. Each opponent is the toughest that you will play—approach games in this way and your players will work hard to reduce their errors to a meaningless few.

A coach can be a good loser and still take defeat badly. You need not take anything away from your opponent's fine play, good fortune or lucky break. Instead, ponder your own team's

GOAL! No feeling like it.

unpreparedness, failure to react to a critical situation, your own poor substituting or underrating of the opponent. This will not be a reflection upon your character as a coach and your players not only will respect you and act in kind, but they will rally with you in preparing for the next game.

A false leader says, "I won," in victory and, "My side lost," in defeat. A real leader says, "My side won," in victory and, "I lost," in defeat.

2

Between the Lines: Field Layout and Equipment

THE PLAYING FIELD

A soccer field is a soccer field, right? Wrong! Soccer fields all come in the same shape, rectangular, but are permitted to be different sizes. The space available and the desired playing surface dictates the dimensions, within a required range of lengths and widths.

The field must be not more than 130 yards and not less than 100 yards long. The width can vary between 50 and 100 yards.

Size of the field is important to the coach, who may have personnel better qualified to perform on a large field than a smaller one. A small field calls for tighter control of the ball and reduces the capability of placing long balls into open spaces to encourage long runs.

It is also important that you as a coach know the dimensions and inner field line markings because you may wind up laying out the field

yourself on occasion. However, a good coach, even at the youth level, will have someone else responsible for preparing the field, so that when you arrive for a game, the focus of your attention can be directed toward preparing your team.

The field should be marked with highly visible lines, using lime or marking powder, no more than five inches wide. The sidelines, called touch lines in soccer, form the boundaries of the field. When the ball leaves the field on the sides, it is returned to play from the point where it went out.

The goal lines at each end complete the rectangle. When the ball crosses the line fully in the air or on the ground between the goalposts, it is a goal. If the ball leaves the field last touched by an offensive player outside the goalposts, it is

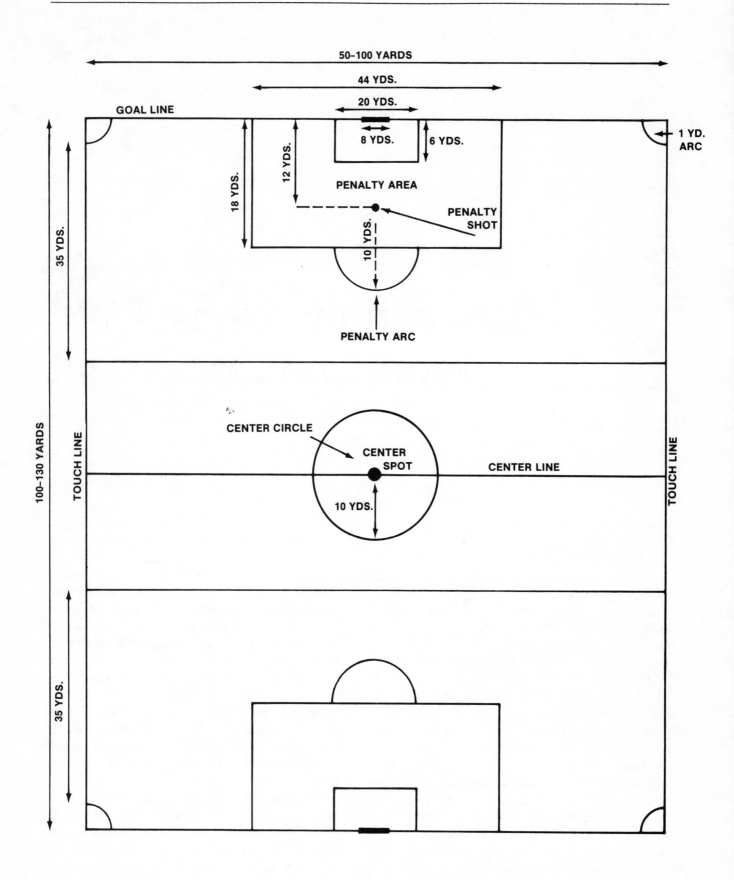

put back into play by a goal kick; if last touched by a defensive player, it is returned to a play by a corner kick.

The center line divides the field into two equal halves. Kickoffs, which occur to start the game, to begin the second half, and following each goal, are executed from the midpoint of this line which is also the determining factor in calling offsides in all of soccer except the North American Soccer League. The kickoff is performed inside a circle with a radius of ten yards, which marks the center of the field. The outside of the circle forms the restraining line for all defending players on the kickoff. The defenders cannot move inside the circle until the ball is moved forward by the kicking team.

In front of the goalposts is a box called the goal area, which reaches six yards into the field and intersects the goal line six yards outside each goal post. Goal kicks are taken from the top of the goal area.

Outside the goal area is a larger box which is the penalty area. This is goalkeeper territory, reaching 18 yards into the field from end line points 18 yards from each goalpost. The goalkeeper, who must obey the rules like other players elsewhere on the field, may handle the ball anywhere inside the penalty area. Kicks taken by the defense, such as goal kicks, must leave this area to be playable.

Direct free kicks charged against the defense for violations inside the penalty area result in a penalty kick, taken from a penalty spot 12 yards from the center of the goal posts.

The only other markings are the corner arcs, lines connecting the end line to the touch line at each corner of the field. This designates the placement of the ball for corner kicks. Flags mark the four corners of the field.

Goal nets are not compulsory, but they are an accessory that should not be omitted. The thrill of seeing the ball land in the back of the net is worth the extra effort required to hang the nets.

Before starting this task, make sure there are hooks, placed several feet apart, on the back side of the goal posts and the cross bar. Suggested aids for putting up the nets are a hammer or rubber mallet, hooked stakes for pinning down the nets behind the goal posts, and a ladder, which relieves wear and tear on shoulders when holding up another person to hook the net along the crossbar.

The goal posts should be white in color so they can easily be seen and the nets should be a different, brighter color, such as orange or green.

TEAM EQUIPMENT

It's no secret that soccer is inexpensive when compared with other sports. No helmets, no shoulder pads, no skates, gloves, or bats. Only a boy (or girl) and a ball are necessary to play the game.

But you're the coach of a team, one that's going to be a winner. It will hardly help your rise to success if your team looks like a loser. If your players are going to be successful, they might as well begin by looking like winners.

Before you start looking for fancy uniforms, though, take stock of your most important needs. Consider practicality and comfort in choosing your team's gear.

The most important part of a player's equipment is his shoes.

Professional teams normally provide shoes, a pair for each type of turf and field condition. Equipment managers look after the shoes and other gear.

On the non-professional level, players usually supply their own shoes. Urge them to seek a good fit and not buy too cheaply. The player probably will find the right shoe only through trial and error. You might counsel him on the type of shoe he should shop for with consideration for the type of field conditions he will have for practice and for games.

On a lush grassy field, the six-cleated shoe is ideal. The cleats are actually interchangeable nylon studs that dig into the ground for good traction. Studs of different lengths and widths can be obtained for different field conditions. For a rough, hard surface, a multi-cleated shoe will be better. These shoes have 13 or 14 small rubber studs on the sole and will provide the player with proper traction and absorb shock better. Traction is vital; a slip by a defender with improper shoes at the wrong time may result in a goal that changes the course of a game.

Players should be advised to regularly check their shoes for loose soles or cleats and for wear and tear, especially inside the shoe where irregularities can produce blisters. Players can get a lot of mileage (you can get your point across by using the term "miles" without exaggerating) from a pair of shoes if they will care for them. A wet cloth or a bit of saddle soap will do wonders for this most vital piece of soccer equipment.

Uniform jerseys can range from a simple T-shirt with a number to more fancy threads, but whatever your team wears, remember that comfort and wearability are most important. Most shirts on the market are made of nylon knit, rayon, dureen, and cotton mixtures. Consider having long sleeves for fall, winter, and spring, and short sleeves for summer or warm climates. The jersey should be fitted for comfort, especially in the neck and chest area.

Shorts are being cut more for speed than protection these days. Years ago, soccer shorts were baggy and reached to the knees, but no more. Nevertheless, they should have plenty of room in the legs to provide freedom of movement.

Uniform sets can be purchased from most sporting goods stores and the North American Soccer League has recently licensed a New York firm to manufacture replicas of the league's team members for a cost as low as $6.00 per set of jersey and shorts.

Most teams wear stockings that have a foot in them like regular socks and reach to just below the knee. Shinguards are optional, but thin, lightweight pads placed under the stockings will protect against sore shins and even cuts and fractures.

Since the goalkeeper is permitted to use his hands and should be distinguishable when cavorting among members of both teams, he is required to wear a jersey of a different color from that of either team. Goalkeepers may also want to wear shorts with hip pads, knee pads and gloves, although many goalies prefer to keep their hands bare for a better feel of the ball. Gloves can come in handy on cold and wet days.

Miscellaneous equipment that will help you do your job as coach include highway marker cones (for dribbling drills or to use as goals for short-sided games), two different colored sets of cloth sashes (bibs) for identifying teams in intrasquad scrimmages, and an air pump. The well-dressed coach may also sport a stop watch, whistle, and clipboard.

Not the least of the gear that should accompany you at all times is a team medical kit. Professional teams have full-time trainers, but you must be prepared for emergency treatment of minor injuries. Standard injury first aid can be abbreviated as I.C.E: Ice, Compression, Elevation. When in doubt, consult a physician. Items in your first aid kit should include:

Adhesive Tape
Ammonia Capsules
Analgesic Balm
Ankle Wraps
Antiseptic Solution
Antiseptic Soap
Aspirin Tablets
Band-Aids
Elastic Bandages
Elastic Tape
Eye Wash
Foot Powder
Petroleum Jelly
Rosin (paste and powder)
Cold Pack
Medicated Ointment
Sterile Pads (Telfa)
Oral Screw
Peroxide
Salt Tablets
Sponge Rubber
Tape Remover
Scissors
Slings

3

Seventeen Commandments: How to Help Your Players through Knowledge of the Rules

For a coach in any sport, the rule book is required reading. It is also imperative that you teach the rules to the players on your team.

For a winning coach in soccer, another step is vital. That is to know how your team can gain an advantage over an opponent through knowledge of the rules. It is amazing how many professional players and coaches lack a full grasp of the laws of the game. It is usually these players and coaches who scream at the referees on every judgment that goes against them. And, at game's end, they blame the officials for the loss that might not have been if they had known, and used, the rules to change the pace of the action.

The rules should not be excuses for losing. Rather, they can and should be tools for victory.

This chapter will deal with the 17 laws of the game and how you can make use of them in your role as a winning coach.

RULE 1

The Field of Play

Elements of this rule were discussed at length in Chapter Two and a diagram details the accepted dimensions.

As a coach, it is your responsibility to regularly check your practice field for ruts, holes, rocks and other potential hazards. Do the same before a game. It is well worth a few extra minutes of your pre-game time to inspect the field for unusual characteristics that you can pass along to your team.

Freshly cut grass will indicate that passes will skim along the ground more quickly than if the grass is higher. Caution your players about unusual areas of the field, such as stretches of dirt that would alter the speed of the ball, soggy spots that might cause a fall or bumpy hazards where controlling the ball would be difficult.

Since the dimensions of a soccer field vary, note the size of each game field. A large pitch provides more space and your players should use wide-open areas to pass and run; a small field will call for tighter control of the ball by your team. The larger the area the better the advantage to the attackers; the smaller the area the more offensive play becomes restricted.

RULE 2

The Ball

The circumference shall not be more than 28 inches and not less than 27 inches. The weight at the start of the game shall not be more than 16 ounces nor less than 14 ounces. The ball shall not be changed during a game unless authorized by the Referee.

While many balls are recommended for training players, only one is needed for a game. Balls are not tossed in and out of the game as in baseball.

Instruct your players to get the "feel" of the ball as soon as possible after the kickoff. Advise them to be aware of a heavier ball in wet weather. Manufacturers have greatly improved the makeup of soccer balls to be more resilient in the toughest weather conditions.

Most teams will use practice balls until they wear out, but as often as possible use the best ball in your possession for practice scrimmages.

Soccer balls will last longer if given good care. If the leather cover looks dry, wash with saddle soap. When used on a wet day, the mud should be removed and the balls properly inflated before drying. After the season is over, balls that are in good condition should be deflated to about half the normal pressure and stored where they will not be crushed or flattened.

RULE 3

Number of Players

Each team consists of 11 players, one of whom must be the goalkeeper.

The number of substitutes permitted is dictated by the rules of the league in which your team plays. In professional games an injured player may be replaced, but once he leaves the field he cannot return to the game.

If a player is ejected from the game for violent conduct or serious foul play, using foul or abusive language or repeated misconduct, he may *not* return to the game. When this occurs, his team plays with ten players.

In many youth and high school leagues, there is unlimited substitution. Substitutes in these leagues may enter the game when their team has possession of the ball when play is stopped, i.e., throw-in, free kick, corner kick, etc., or after a goal has been scored by either team.

Players generally are grouped on the field in three basic units—defenders, midfielders and forwards. The eleventh man is the goalkeeper, the only player permitted to use his hands on the ball.

The goalkeeper, of course, is stationed in front of the goal. The remaining players may be aligned in any way the coach wishes. Basically, however, a team starts with either four defenders, three midfielders, and three forwards (4-3-3 in soccer terminology); or three defenders, three midfielders, and four forwards (3-3-4).

These positions may be called by different names and a coach probably will use more specific designations when he begins assigning players to positions. Defenders become fullbacks, centerbacks, sweeper, stopper; midfielders become halfbacks or linkmen; forwards become strikers or insides and wings.

The goalkeeper normally remains inside the penalty area, since when he leaves it he no longer has special dispensation to use his hands.

In front of him are the defenders. A special pride should develop among these backs, and close communication between them and the goalkeeper should exist since they, as a group, are charged with keeping the enemy from penetrating the goal.

Connecting the play between the forwards and defense are midfielders, who range up and down the field concentrating on attack or defense depending on the position of the ball. The area that these players patrol is often referred to as the engine room because a team's attack is generated by the success achieved here.

Up front, the men generally responsible for getting goals are the forwards. Their main duty is to score. In the forward line there is usually a striker or center forward who often plays with his back to the goal, somewhat like a pivot man in basketball, so that he may spin and cut in the direction of the ball being passed into him or to follow up on shots taken by the wing forwards.

Systems of play and responsibilities of players at specific positions will be discussed at greater length in later chapters.

RULE 4

Player Equipment

Consists of a shirt, shorts, stockings, and shoes. Goalkeeper must wear colors which distinguish him from the other players.

See Chapter Three.

RULE 5

Referees

One referee is appointed for each match. He is responsible for control of the game and his decisions are final.

That's referee with a capital "R." He is charged with the responsibility of administering the rules of the game. He is given wide powers to exercise proper control and he is the sole judge of any disputed incident.

Soccer, perhaps more than any other sport, allows the referee to make calls which may appear contrary to the stated rule. The referee may decide whether an infraction is intentional or accidental; he may refuse to whistle a clear violation if stoppage of play would take the advantage from the offended team.

As a coach, you have certain responsibilities to the referee. See that your team is ready to play on time. Respect his decisions. Do not enter the field under any circumstances, except when permission has been granted to attend an injured player. Instruct your players to play the game and leave the officiating to the referee. Do not try to intimidate a referee. He's human, and the less you irritate him, the better it's going to be for you and your team.

RULE 6

Linesmen

Two linesmen assist the referee by indicating offside, when the ball is out of play, and which team is entitled to the corner kick or throw in.

The linesmen operate along the outside of the touchlines, each with a flag for signaling off-sides violations and out-of-play situations, which result in a throw-in or corner kick. They work in cooperation with the referee, who has the final decision on all calls. Often the referee, even if he has not observed an offsides violation, will act on the linesman's call and cancel a goal. Each linesman normally works one-half of the field, permitting the referee to operate on a diagonal line on the field. This usually results in at least one, and sometimes two, officials to be near the play wherever it occurs.

Even though the referee is in command, always treat the linesmen with the same respect and instruct your players to do the same.

RULE 7

Duration of the Game

Shall be two equal periods of 45 minutes unless otherwise agreed upon.

The normal period of play is 90 minutes, divided by a 5- to 15-minute halftime. In youth leagues, especially for players under 12 years of age, equal halves of 30 minutes are played.

The referee is the sole timekeeper and he will stop his watch only to allow an injured player to receive treatment or for a penalty kick. He may also stop time for some lengthy delay such as a ball leaving the field and entering the stands. The referee is responsible for adding time to compensate for the amount of time lost.

On many levels of play, games that are dead-locked after regulation play are scored as ties. In some leagues, two overtime periods of from five to ten minutes each are added to break the ties and if the game remains tied, a series of alternating penalty kicks are taken to reach a verdict.

North American Soccer League games which

are tied at the end of regulation play are extended by 15 minutes of sudden death overtime (two 7½-minute periods). If no score occurs in the first period, the teams change ends of the field for the second overtime period. If the game remains deadlocked, the outcome is decided by a system called The Shootout, which involves players on each team challenging the opposing goalkeeper in a one-on-one situation. The kicks continue in alternating fashion until one team has achieved an insurmountable advantage.

A winning coach will always be aware of the time remaining in the half or in the game. This will assist him in making substitutions and also in determining his placement of players in situations where the score may call for an attacking style of play or a defensive-minded game.

RULE 8

The Start of Play

A flip of coin decides which team will kick off. Each team must stay on its own half of the field and the defending players must be at least 10 yards from the ball until it is kicked. After a goal the team scored upon will kick off. After halftime the teams change ends and the kickoff will be taken by the opposite team to that which started the game. A goal cannot be scored directly from a kickoff.

To some coaches, the kickoff at the beginning of a game and at halftime are mere formalities. To the winning coach, it is an advantage situation that should not be thrown away. True, a team at the kickoff never has more opponents between itself and the goal and plays are more difficult to execute. While this may reduce the amount of success you can expect, it should by no means stifle planning of plays off the kickoff. While the plays should be simple, every player on the team should know what is about to happen, even if it involves only two or three players.

Nothing could be simpler than the kickoff play that has been used occasionally by world-class teams, playing the ball back to a wing midfielder, who boots a long, curved ball into the opposing penalty area. The element of surprise, in addition to the flurry of forwards pouring past standing defenders, was plenty to shock the opponent into confusion at the outset of a game.

RULE 9

Ball In and Out of Play

The ball is out of play when (a) it has wholly crossed the goal line or touchline, whether on the ground or in the air, or (b) when the game has been stopped by the referee.

Instruct your players: "Always believe the referee is going to do what you want him to do." Never anticipate the whistle.

Make certain your players understand that the ball isn't out of play until it *completely crosses* the touchlines. Instruct your players not to relax in their pursuit of a ball when it nears the touchline. Let the opponent give up . . . it will give your man an extra second and extra space to make a pass that will gain or maintain possession.

Throw-ins are another re-start of play that should be taken seriously. Some referees will insist on their whistle re-starting the play when the ball is out-of-bounds, but players should presume that he is not going to blow his whistle and make the throw-in as quickly as possible. The sooner you can get a numerical advantage against a team, the better chance you have to convert a re-start into a scoring opportunity.

The same philosophy exists on free kicks. Take them quickly. However, a quick kick is useless unless the kicker's teammates are on their toes and thinking, too.

Coach your team to react defensively on these plays, too. A sleeping defense becomes the victim of the very things you are teaching to your attackers.

RULE 10

Method of Scoring

A goal is scored when the whole of the ball has passed over the goal line, between the goal posts and under the cross bar.

The sight of Pele leaping into the air with his

THROW-IN: Wrong way and . . .

THROW-IN: Right way.

fist reaching for the sky needs only one caption: "Goal!" Scoring goals is the aim in soccer and players need little prodding from a coach to know what it's all about. "Put it in the back of the net" needs no elaboration.

Defensively, though, a word should be impressed upon your team. Again, the important phrase is "has passed over the goal line." That means *completely* over the goal line.

For the goalkeeper, that means no surrendering a ball that is close. And many a quick-thinking defender has snuffed out an opponent's scoring opportunity when his goalkeeper has been drawn off the line. A defender standing inside the goal can kick out a shot before it enters the goal.

RULE 11

Offside

A player is offside if he is nearer his opponents' goal line than the ball at the moment the ball is played unless, (a) he is in his own half of the field of play, (b) there are two of his opponents nearer to their own goal line than he is, (c) the ball last touched an opponent or was last played by him or (d) he receives the ball direct from a goal kick, a corner kick, a throw in, or when it was dropped by the referee.

NOTE: This is the traditional rule. In 1973 the NASL introduced a "Blue Line" concept with a line drawn the width of the field 35 yards

HANDS: This one is intentional . . .

. . . but the referee may allow this unintentional one.
Handling ball is penalized by direct free kick.

from each goal. Under this rule, an attacking player is not offside until he is within 35 yards of his opponents' goal rather than midfield, as under the traditional rule.

This is the most cantankerous of the rules soccer lives by. Rather simply stated, a player must have two opponents, the goalkeeper and another player, between himself and the goal when the ball is played unless he is accompanied by the ball.

However, since you are a winning coach, your players will know that they can receive the ball from a throw-in while in an offside position. If your opponents are unsure of this, it might mean a goal. In fact, a player cannot be offside on a goal kick, corner kick, or drop ball either. However, once the ball has been played on a teammate, he must be prepared to return onside if he isn't the recipient of the ball.

A player is usually not penalized for being in an offside position unless in the opinion of the referee he is interfering with the play or an opponent, or is seeking to gain an advantage by being offside.

RULE 12

Fouls and Misconduct

A player who intentionally attempts to or actually: (1) kicks, (2) trips, (3) jumps at, (4) charges violently, (5) charges from behind, (6) strikes, (7) holds, or (8) pushes an opponent, or (9) intentionally handles the ball shall be penalized by a direct free kick. Any one of these nine offenses committed in the penalty area by a defender will result in a penalty kick to the offensive team.

A player committing less flagrant violations such as offside, dangerous plays, obstruction, or ungentlemanly conduct will be penalized by an indirect free kick.

Teach your players to avoid unnecessary fouls. Many are committed simply because a player was not concentrating on his responsibilities. A player will sometimes attempt a tackle when there's obviously no chance to connect with the ball. A trip occurs and the player's team is penalized. The referee usually will rely on his opinion as to whether to call a foul. See that your players understand this and don't dispute his calls when they occur against your team.

tion of the rules, yelling and screaming won't help. He should file a protest to league officials following the game.

RULE 13
Free Kicks

Are classified into two categories: "Direct" (from which a goal can be scored directly against the offending side) and "Indirect" (from which a goal cannot be scored unless the ball has been touched by a player other than the kicker before entering the goal). For all free kicks the offending team must be at least 10 yards from the ball until it is kicked.

Advise your players that a direct free kick does not have to be taken directly at the goal. The defensive team must be at least 10 yards from the ball on a free kick, but if it has set up a well-positioned wall, a teammate stationed nearer the kicker cannot be marked closely and may have a clear shot on goal when he receives the ball.

Setting up a compact defensive wall.

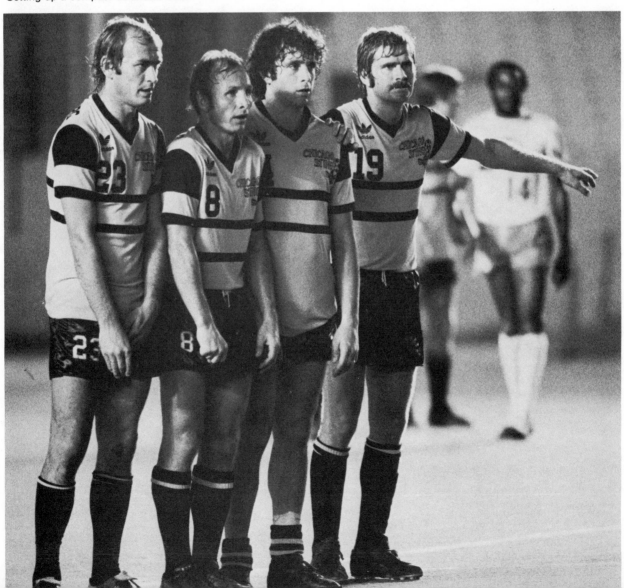

Instruct your players to take up the ten yards distance on defense. Don't try to intimidate the referee by trying to set up the wall less than ten yards away.

RULE 14

Penalty Kick

A direct free kick taken at the penalty mark. All players except the player taking the kick and the goalkeeper must stay outside the penalty area and at least 10 yards from the ball (hence the arc at edge of penalty area).

Your penalty taker should be an accurate kicker who can stay cool and relaxed under pressure. His responsibility is to score a goal. Since he must keep the ball away from the goalkeeper with a hard enough kick to beat the keeper's lunge, he should disguise the direction of his kick until the last moment. He should fix the type of kick he will use in his mind and not change at the last moment. This usually winds up as a shot directly at the goalkeeper. The kicker's teammates should be prepared to handle a rebound since the kicker is not permitted a second kick at the ball until it has been played by another player.

Defensively, the backs should try to get inside positions on the attacking players in order to obstruct their rush for a rebound. The defending team forwards should drop back to receive clearing kicks or passes from the penalty area.

Some say the goalkeeper should rub his rabbit's foot and take a guess which way the kick is coming. This is partially true since a penalty kick is converted about eight times out of ten by the kicker. Teach your goalkeeper to be observant and he may pick up a tendency by the kicker. Or he may just decide the way he's going

THROW-IN: Both hands must propel the ball equally. Here's the right way . . .

. . . and the wrong way.

to dive by the way the kicker runs up to the ball.

An average penalty kick travels the 12-yard distance in five hundredths of a second. Any stop by the goalkeeper is gold.

RULE 15

Throw In

> When the ball has wholly crossed the touchline it is put back into play by a throw in from the spot where it went out and by a player from the opposite team that last touched it. A goal cannot be scored directly from a throw in.

The thrower must face the field of play and the ball must be delivered from behind and over the head with both hands equally propelling the ball. Both feet must be either on the touchline or outside upon delivery.

Sound simple? In non-professional games teams regularly lose possession due to poor throw-ins. Stress proper methods of throw-ins during practices and require that they are taken properly. It is vital that the throw-in be taken quickly when the opponent isn't concentrating. Stress the importance of the throw-in to your players—it's the start of an offensive opportunity and should not be thrown away due to carelessness.

RULE 16

Goal Kick

> When the ball has wholly crossed the goal line after being last touched by a player from the attacking team, it is put back into play by a kick from the goal area by the defending team.

The goal kick, too, is the beginning of an attacking opportunity and it is essential that all eleven players are thinking that way. A little forethought may enable the kicker to drop the ball into an area occupied only by a teammate. Sometimes it is beneficial to make a short pass outside the penalty area (goal kicks must clear the penalty area before anyone from either team may touch the ball) to a defender, who returns it to the goalkeeper, who then can punt it downfield or pass to a defender. This is dangerous if mishandled, so practice time on the short goal kick is vital.

RULE 17

Corner Kick

> When the ball has wholly crossed the goal line after being last touched by a player from the defending team, it is put back into play by a kick from the corner on the side the ball went out by the attacking team.

Most corner kicks are long crosses into the goal mouth. An effective changeup, and sometimes especially effective on the youth level, is the short corner. Since the opponent must be at least ten yards from the kicker, a player on the attacking team may position himself close by to receive a pass unmarked by an opponent. The kicker, however, must remember that once the first pass has been made, he becomes subject to the offside rule. He may either immediately rush on side or step off the field until the ball has been played elsewhere on the field.

4
Teaching Techniques: Ball Control, Trapping, Dribbling, Passing, Heading, Tackling . . .

A leader is best
when people barely know he exists
Not so good
when people obey and acclaim him.
Worse when they despise him.
But of a good leader
who talks little
when his work is done
his aim fulfilled
they will say:
"We did it ourselves."

—Lao-Tse

You are reading this book, we hope, to become not a famous coach, but a successful one.

Good coaching is good teaching, and getting down to the nitty-gritty basics with the proper enthusiasm and attention to detail is sometimes difficult for any coach, whatever his experience.

Without ever losing sight that soccer is a game of teamwork, you must realize that it all begins with basic skills—you cannot have team tactics unless players first master the basic techniques.

Some coaches operate on the theory that because soccer is a team game, all teaching begins with organized play and that skills will be developed in the context of the team's game.

This doesn't always ring true. Teaching skills is vital—the player who is taught from an early age that there are many ways to manipulate a ball and the proper methods of performance will become increasingly useful to his team. With proper instruction, he will learn to concentrate on mastering the skills of shooting, passing, dribbling, heading, screening, trapping, and tackling with every moment of his free time instead of frittering it away on horseplay.

You as a coach must cultivate an interest in

Despite defender's efforts, Sting's Dick Advocaat keeps him from ball.

the player to get things done, and done the right way. He will develop an urgent need to move from one point to another, to rise to a specific goal. He will enjoy using his newfound skills and be excited when they are put to the test.

As often as facilities and situations permit, training should begin with each boy having a ball of his own with which to practice. If that's not possible, then three boys to a ball, or four, so that they might participate in skill practices which will give them constant contact with the bwl.

It has been determined that in an average 90-minute game, a player has possession from two and a half to five minutes.

Some players will control the ball more than others, but the point is that the smaller the group of players using a ball the more time each will have to get the feel of it.

One boy with one ball, then, will have even more opportunity to master the skills. He can practice bringing it under control by kicking it against a wall or by throwing the ball into the air. While he may be hesitant out of shyness or embarrassment to use his weak foot in an or-

ganized drill, he will force himself to learn to kick with both feet in his own private sessions so that he can show it off in team practices.

The way the game is developing, every player, with the possible exception of the goalkeeper, should be able to master these skills because every player should be able to play every position on the field. Defenders, as well as forwards and midfielders, should be skillful at every aspect of the game.

The first step for the player in learning to perform the skill properly is getting a mental image by use of diagrams, demonstrations, and word descriptions of how it should be executed. It is important for the coach to give his players as clear a picture as possible of the movements involved.

The second step is practice, without opposition. Slow motion movements are helpful at first, then the skill should be repeated with increasing speed, making sure the correct form is followed. Some players will progress faster than others, but the slow learners should not be rushed at this stage. Working in small groups of three or four, either passing among themselves. or advancing toward the goal, they will gain confidence.

The third step is using the skill in game situations, against opposition. At first the player should work in small groups with staged situations that will arise in a game, beginning with small pressure from the opposition and gradually building into stronger and more aggressive defense.

PASSING

The key to victory is passing. It is the chain link in the road to the goal. Teach your players to pass well and your chances of success improve with each touch of the ball. Bad passing surrenders possession of the ball *and* control of the game.

It is the most basic skill in soccer and yet it is so varied and so vital that it remains the most difficult to teach. It is the heart of perfect teamwork. Good passing will lift the confidence of players in their teammates. Ballhogging will be reduced if players know they will get the ball back when they give it up.

There are three important factors in accurate

Jorgen Kristensen uses outside of his foot to control ball.

passing: the passer, the ball and the receiver.

The *passer* should conceal his intentions until the last possible moment, never telegraphing his passes. After bringing the ball under control, he must look up to see an open teammate, then look down at the ball while making the pass. He should pass to open space in front of the receiver before making the pass.

It is the duty of the passer to find space after passing the ball by shaking off the opponent marking him and get into position to again receive the ball.

The *ball* should be "weighted" properly, that is, have the correct amount of speed. A pass on the ground should be rolling and not bouncing and should lead the receiver. A high hard pass to a nearby teammate restricts his ability to control it as does a slow pass that will not reach him.

The *receiver* should maneuver into a position to collect the pass by getting between the man marking him and the ball or by running into space. He should run to meet the ball, taking a quick glance at the field of play as the ball is traveling toward him. This will enable him to decide what he will do with the ball, then look again at the ball as he receives it. It is important that the ball is played again quickly.

There are as many types of passes as there are ways to maneuver into a position to deliver effective passes as the player grows in experience.

The most important technique in short passing is also probably the easiest to coach—the inside-of-the-foot pass. It is also the easiest to execute with accuracy.

The inside-of-the-foot pass is delivered with a pushing action, using the part of the foot between the big toe and the heel. The leg is swung from the hip with the ankle locked and a smooth follow-through is vital. The non-kicking foot should be planted slightly behind the ball.

A variation is the outside-of-the-foot pass which permits more deception. This is executed with a flick of the foot, using the outside of the instep and swinging the leg away from the body. Again, the follow-through is important.

For longer passing, the instep is used. This is the most important part of the foot for long passing and shooting and perhaps the most difficult to coach. Young players are reluctant to use the instep and, even when they surrender to learning it, find it difficult to achieve the proper form for accurate kicks.

The instep pass is executed by placing the non-kicking foot alongside the ball, swinging the kicking leg forward from the hip and at the same time bending the knee so the heel is well behind the body. The leg is straightened when the knee comes in line with the ball and the eye. The ball is struck with the top of the instep, with the shoelaces, and the toe is down and extended. The head and body should be over the ball and not leaning back. The muscles of the leg should be relaxed until the kick is started and the ankle should remain relaxed until the moment of impact with the ball, at which time it is locked. The power of the kick comes from the knee, not the hip. A well-executed instep kick will produce a ball with backspin and, if the toes are kept pointing downward, will remain low in flight.

A variation of the instep kick is the volley, which can be used in passing, shooting or clear-

English International Gordon Hill scores again.

An aggressive volley kick, clearing ball from danger.

ing from a dangerous position when there is no time to control the ball.

To volley-kick a ball is to kick it while it is in the air either before or after it bounces. This is a tough skill to master, but can be very effective for the player who has the patience and persistence. The ball is hit with the instep and the success of the kick depends almost entirely on keeping the eye on the ball until it meets the foot. The nearer the ground the ball, the lower it will be in flight. Beginners have a tendency to get into position for the kick too soon and consequently misjudge the flight of the ball. The player must be ready to change his stance until the last second.

It is generally believed that the most important pass in soccer is the final pass before a

goal. Make sure that player who delivers the final pass receives the recognition he deserves. In professional soccer, he is awarded an assist and one point in individual scoring totals. In nonprofessional ranks, he often goes undetected and, even if he is noticed, his glory is short-lived. Make sure that player gets a word or two of praise from you, the coach. Let him know you recognize his contribution to the goal.

But emphasize to your players that *every* pass is important. Attention to this will prevent a lot of mid-field carelessness.

Mastering these techniques in passing leads your players into the fun area of soccer—shooting.

SHOOTING

The most glamorous part of the game is scoring goals and there's no reason why shooting should not be given early attention. Practicing shots on goal not only is fun, but learning to kick with power and finesse prepares the young player to develop the touch he needs for passing techniques that lead up to scoring opportunities.

The basic rules for kicking:

Place the non-kicking foot alongside the ball, making sure the kicking leg is not stretching to hit the ball. Keep the head still and over the ball, eyes on the ball. As the kicking leg swings forward, weight of the body should shift to the non-kicking leg. The ball should be met with the top of the instep. The kicking leg should follow through, with the toe extended or pointed downward.

These mechanics will give the ball a backspin and keep it low. The power and accuracy needed to put it past the goalkeeper will come with practice.

As the player masters this basic kick, he will find that he can accomplish marvelous things with subtle changes in the mechanics. Turning the toe of the kicking foot slightly in or out will cause a sideward spin and the ball will bend, or curve. Placing the non-kicking foot slightly behind the ball will cause it to rise and when combined with power will result in a long kick. Lifting the toe of the kicking foot upon impact will make the ball rise steeply, useful in chipping over an opponent.

The potential goal-scorer soon learns that the ball is not set out on a silver platter (except on a penalty kick when strict adherence to the broad rule discussed above is essential), so that he becomes more proficient in using variations and improvisations when confronted with game situations.

There are scoring opportunities, for example, when the shooter doesn't have time to swing his leg in a full arc to get off the shot. The ball would either be stolen by a defender or, in close quarters, the leg would strike another player on the backswing. This calls for a short backswing and a swift, hard kick.

Two principles that you cannot over-emphasize to your players are broad rules that apply in most all sports—*keep your eye on the ball and follow-through.*

BALL CONTROL

Teach trapping and dribbling under the umbrella title of ball control, for it is mastering these skills that enable the player to get into position to pass and shoot.

Good ball control is aided and abetted by the ability to juggle—that is, to keep a ball in the air with feet, thighs, chest and head—or to balance the ball on the instep for long periods. But that is only the beginning and these are skills that the player should practice individually before and after practice. Achievement of these skills will depend on a player's desire to get the feel of the ball or to perform tricks like a circus seal.

But the nitty-gritty of ball control comes down to collecting the ball by various methods

Looking for a teammate without breaking stride while dribbling.

Proper kicking form. Note non-kicking foot alongside ball, arms extended for balance, knee bent, eyes on the ball.

of trapping and by being able to do something with the ball immediately after bringing it under control.

Trapping

The first fundamental of trapping is the decision about which surface of the body, chest, thigh, foot, etc., to use to meet the ball.

Secondly, that surface should be relaxed and withdrawn just before the ball makes impact and while impact is made to produce a cushion-like effect.

Regardless of the experience of your players, much time and effort should be spent on trapping. The coach should insist that all balls in practice be trapped or brought under control before they are played, except when practicing one-touch passing and kicking.

The ball is properly trapped when it stops dead at the foot or within one step of the player. The player should be taught early that if the ball does not stop dead, the player should immediately go to the ball and do whatever it is he wants to do with it. He should *never*, in drill, scrimmage, or game, stand flat-footed when a ball is loose.

Basic traps are made with the inside, outside, and sole of the foot, the chest and the thigh.

The principles in all these traps remain the same.

1. Face the oncoming ball.
2. Judge the flight of the ball.
3. Decide which surface of the body will be used to meet the ball.
4. Keep the eye on the ball.
5. Relax the part of the body being used.
6. Keep arms extended for balance.
7. Be ready to advance the ball under control.

Sting's Arno Steffenhagen stretches for outside-of-the-foot trap.

TRAPPING: Outside of the foot trap.

TRAPPING: Inside of the foot trap.

Instruct your players that once they have received a ball, it is theirs and that they should not let it go until they are ready to give it up. They must not permit an opponent to win the ball while it is being trapped.

Players will soon learn that the better their ability to control the ball, the more often their teammates will want to pass the ball to them, knowing that it will be in safe hands . . . or rather, feet.

Dribbling

Dribbling is a fine art that, properly honed, can provide a devastating weapon in a team's offensive arsenal. Improperly used, it can also be a killer of team play. Pure dribblers win or lose spectacularly and, unless they learn what is the opportune moment to deliver a pass, will wreck attacking thrusts and scoring opportunities.

The Chicago Sting has been fortunate to have employed two of the finest dribblers of a soccer ball in the world during the team's tenure, each with his own distinctive style. Gordon Hill, now an International star in England, played with the Sting in 1975 and wreaked havoc among NASL defenders. He relies on speed and

Making a chest trap.

Chicago Sting's Jorgen Kristensen has his defender going one way as he prepares to go the other.

Self-improvement exercise . . . juggling with the thigh.

strength to push past opponents, allowing the ball to run, but tenaciously holding onto it. Jorgen Kristensen, the great Danish International currently with the Sting, appears to have the ball tied to his toe as he turns defenders inside out with unbelievable balance and control.

Dribbling, then, is running with the ball under control, and players who master the skill will be able to take on defenders and beat them. It is probably the most creative of skills and once you have imparted the basics, you will be wise to encourage players to develop their own tricks to move the ball.

You will be able to judge which players have a knack for the skill of dribbling with simple relay races and moving the ball around cones in a

line. But too much concentration on these drills will be wasted time, since the player needs to be encouraged to develop body movement and changes in direction and speed.

Most players will begin dribbling using the inside of their feet, but the best way for them to run with the ball under control is to turn their feet inward and push the ball forward with the outside of the foot. This will enable the player to run with little change in his running stride and reduce the number of times he touches the ball, also enabling him to stop quickly and accelerate just as quickly. Encourage players to collect a moving ball when they start dribbling rather than a still ball.

Encourage the player to develop full vision while he is dribbling rather than charging

Sting's Arno Steffenhagen dribbling ball upfield quickly.

blindly forward with the ball. Running in a figure eight route helps to develop sharp turns using both inside and outside of the feet; and exercises that stress sidewise movement and running backwards, then forward, will help to develop the feints and body movement necessary.

HEADING

In no sport does the command, "use your head," have a more literal meaning than in soccer.

Heading a soccer ball is an awkward business at best and one of the most difficult skills to teach, but the player who masters it will add a new dimension to his overall value to the team.

For the forward who is good in the air, it will mean more opportunities to score goals. The midfielders will find that they are able to exploit space in the air for long or short passes and defenders will propel balls out of danger that they otherwise would fail to handle at all.

You must help young players overcome the natural fear of the ball striking the head by showing patience and teaching the skill of heading at a slower pace than all other skills. Even

discussing the subject will turn off beginning players.

First, you should show them that there is only one way to head a ball. That is with the center of the forehead at the hairline.

Work with them individually or have teammates toss soft high balls to each other, so they will learn that when headed properly, it will not hurt.

Secondly, emphasize that the ball doesn't hit the player. The player hits the ball.

Using the proper portion of the head, he should strike at the ball with his neck muscles flexed to thrust the head forward. Show the player that direction of the ball will be determined by the part of the ball that is struck, not by the portion of the head.

And finally, that old axiom used with all skills in all sports, keep the eye on the ball until impact.

As the player gets more comfortable with the ball, he will gain confidence and learn how to direct passes to teammates, either high or low.

Jumping ability and timing now comes into play and can make the difference on what is called a "50-50" ball, that is a ball in the air that can be controlled by either team.

Playing ball in air: rising above opponents is important.

Good body position protects the ball from oncoming opponent.

HEADING PRACTICE: Note arms out for balance, eyes on the ball.

TACKLING

Even on defense, your players should be thinking attack. Learning to tackle well will enable defending players to take the initiative against the man with the ball, who starts with all the advantages on his side.

A player does not always win the ball when he tackles, but he has served well if he stops the dribble, forces the opponent to lose control of the ball or forces him to make a bad pass.

In teaching tackling, stress to your players:

1. Always make the man with the ball cause the ball to move.
2. Time your movements so that you tackle just as opponent plays ball.
3. Face the opponent.
4. Concentrate entirely on the ball. The opponent can't go anywhere without it.

SLIDING TACKLE: Tackler must be certain he can get his foot on the ball; otherwise he's down and out of play.

5. Approach the man with the ball from an angle that will prevent him from going where he wants to go if you miss the tackle.
6. The body should be crouched, with arms slightly extended for balance, legs close enough together that the ball can't be played through, but wide enough that the body weight is balanced.

Knowing *when* to tackle is perhaps just as important as knowing how to tackle. This skill will be gained through experience, and practice will help overcome the natural fear, or timidness, of going against the opponent in close combat.

Simple one-on-one and two-on-two drills, with a small goal as an incentive for the dribbler, are effective training methods for tackling.

A last word on tackling. Discourage slide tackling: it should be for desperate circumstances. Good tacklers remain on their feet, think fast, and strike quickly.

5

No Rest for the Weary: Conditioning—In Season and Out

A young man was hitchhiking in the Tennessee mountains and got a lift from an elderly hillbilly gentleman. After driving along for a few miles, the old man suddenly pulled a pistol and ordered his startled young rider: "Look in that compartment there and pull out that fruit jar. Now screw the lid off. Now, take a drink."

The hitchhiker swallowed a drink of 100-proof mountain sugar corn moonshine and began coughing and pounding the dashboard. The old man handed him the pistol and said, "Okay, Bub, now make me take one!"

Soccer players sometimes identify with fitness the way the old man did with his moonshine. They want it, but ask to be forced to undergo the pain that goes with it.

So you, the coach, are expected to put the gun to their heads. When they have reached their threshold of fatigue and long to call it a day, you must demand that they do more.

This "plus" will reduce fatigue to a minimum and increase the chances for victory. Sports are replete with incidents of top class teams, or individuals, suffering defeat to a third-rater who was in better condition. In soccer, an average team in good condition will defeat a good team with mediocre fitness.

Soccer players must be in superior condition. No other game demands as much running, along with other physical exertion like leaping and diving and quick stops and starts—no matter what position is played. Enough conditioning work must be provided so that players will not tire excessively during games.

At the very young levels, the running provided in practices and games will be enough, but as players move into their teens, there should be a gradual increase in the amount of fitness work. In the late teens and early 20's, a player should be involved in graduated stress.

This systematic, graduated stress, whether it involves goal-oriented running, stretching exercises, progressive weight-training, or any combination of these, is simply a way of using our body's natural reaction.

What is conditioning?

Dick Hoover, Head Trainer for the Chicago Sting, and Educational Director of Northwestern University Medical School's Center for Sports Medicine, defines it as "a proper or healthy state of the individual, an ability to rise to meet the situation at hand."

"That situation," says Hoover, "may be the kick to score the winning goal. These situations are the reasons for spending time on a program which will help to meet the challenges as they occur. Conditioning means activity. It is impossible to achieve and maintain a well-conditioned state without working hard.

"Records are made to be broken; the reason for some of these achievements most certainly lies in the conditioning programs which are now much more prevalent than they once were.

"Success (the mark of a champion) is what we are all reaching for, but it is not easy to obtain. Success precedes work only in the dictionary."

The results of good conditioning include an increase in speed, strength, endurance, flexibility and an improvement in coordination and agility. Additionally, there will be an improvement in general health and self-confidence.

A conditioning program, too, aids in the prevention of injuries. Rehabilitative exercises for the knee have proved that muscular strength can be substituted for some joint weaknesses.

Few young people have the desire to attain the degree of physical fitness demanded of athletes. Here's where you, the coach, ride into town with your gun. The soccer player will swallow it at gunpoint and thank you for it later, for it will make a winner out of him and his team.

Much fitness training can be accomplished with drills using the ball in practices. If you must have your players run laps, have them dribble a ball along with them. Sprinting drills, too, can be conducted with the player using a ball.

The coach of a youth team greeted his new players on the first day of practice by ordering a lap around the field. When they finished, he gathered them around him and said: "Now you know the size of the field. That will be the last lap you'll take while I'm coach. I want soccer players, not laprunners. I have other forms of discipline. From now on, we'll do all our running up and down *inside* that area you just lapped." It helped greatly in the behavior of his team. None of the youngsters wanted to find out what other disciplinary methods he had up his sleeve.

Most professional teams do a certain amount of cross-country running and hill climbing in pre-season training. This activity not only strengthens the leg muscles but, more importantly, builds up the player's cardio-respiratory capacity.

As the season draws nearer, distances should be gradually reduced and more sprinting introduced. One excellent drill can be built around the markings on the soccer pitch. It starts slowly with quick starts and stops and builds gradually.

1. Sprint from the goal-line to the six-yard box and return. Do the same distance jogging.
2. Sprint from the goal-line to the 18-yard box and return. Do the same distance jogging.
3. Sprint from the goal-line to the midfield line and jog back.
4. Sprint from the midfield to the six-yard box and return.
5. Sprint from the midfield line to the 18-yard box and return.
6. Sprint from the midfield line to the goal-line and jog back.

There are other programs that should be undertaken under your direction to build up stamina and strength, lack of fatigue, and victories.

Interval training has proved to be an excellent method of conditioning to improve cardio-respiratory efficiency and the development of endurance. It consists of a series of specific work loads interspersed with a series of specific rest periods. The rest periods are not a complete cessation of activity, but a period of walking or jogging.

Until recently, conditioning programs have concentrated on speed, strength, and endurance, ignoring the importance of flexibility.

Such programs tended to restrict normal ranges of motion and build tight, bulky muscles, producing awkward and jerky movements.

Tight muscles cause pressure on the capillaries and slow the blood flow, thereby preventing oxygen from reaching the cells and accumulated fatigue products from being carried away.

These muscles, in addition to being unable to contract properly, lose their ability to relax. These factors combine to make the muscle more prone to injury.

A daily program of flexibility training, lasting ten minutes or less, will enable your players to perform more efficiently and reduce the chances of pulled and strained muscles. It can also aid in improving the speed, quickness, and agility of players.

Following is a program of 17 exercises used by the Chicago Sting in flexibility training. The exercises must be progressive in nature in that the force exerted must be increased gradually and the duration of the hold position must be progressively lengthened with each session. Precautions should be taken to avoid bobbing or up-and-down motions.

Stretching exercises to improve flexibility:

Exercise 1

Purpose: To stretch the hamstring and low back extensor muscles.

Starting Position: Stand with the feet three to four inches apart and parallel to each other.

Movement: Bend forward from the waist and keep the knees straight. Reach toward the floor as far as possible. Let the arms, trunk, and head hang freely. Stretch until the stretch pain is felt. Hold the position three to five seconds. Return to the starting position.

Progression: Do the exercise three times and increase one time every other exercise period until five.

Precautions: Keep the knees straight throughout the movement. Do not use a bobbing motion. Do not overstretch.

Exercise 2

Purpose: To stretch the hamstring, low back extensor and the rotator muscles, and iliotibial band.

Starting Position: Stand, cross the right leg over the left leg and assume a position of stability. Place the right hand on the left shoulder and place the left arm across the small of the back.

Movement: Bend forward from the waist and keep the left knee stabilized with the right leg. Let the head and trunk hang freely. Rotate in the direction of the right leg. Stretch until a stretch pain is felt. Hold the position three to five seconds and return to the starting position. Do alternately.

Progression: Do the exercise three times to each side and increase one time every other exercise period until five.

Precautions: Be sure the base of support is wide enough to maintain balance. Keep the left leg straight. Do not use a jerking or bobbing motion.

Exercise 3

Purpose: To stretch the hamstring muscles, the low back extensor muscles, and the rotator muscles.

Starting Position: Stand at the side of a table or bench at approximately crotch level. Place the leg nearest table on top of table and let the opposite leg hang freely.

Movement: From this position, bend forward at the waist and let the head hang freely. Reach toward the outside of the foot of the extended leg. Stretch until a pain is felt. Hold the position three to five seconds and return to starting position.

Progression: Do the exercise three times to each side and increase one time every other exercise period until five.

Precautions: Keep the extended leg straight. Do not use a jerking or bobbing motion.

Exercise 4

Purpose: To stretch the hamstring muscle.

Starting Position: Sit with the legs extended and the arms outstretched.

Movement: Bend forward from the waist and attempt to reach beyond the toes. Stretch until a stretch pain is felt. Hold the position three to five seconds and return to the starting position.

Progression: Do the exercise three times and

increase one time every other exercise period until five.

Precautions: Do not let the knees bend during the stretch. Do not use a bobbing motion.

Exercise 5

Purpose: To stretch the back extensor muscles.

Starting Position: Sit in a tailor position with the arms folded across the chest.

Movement: Roll the chin on the chest and in a curling motion attempt to touch the forehead to the knees. Hold this position for three to five seconds and return to starting position.

Progression: Do the exercise three times and increase one time every other exercise period until five.

Precautions: Keep the knees level throughout the movement. Do not use a bobbing motion. Do not overstretch. Do not allow the hips to rise from the mat.

Exercise 6

Purpose: To stretch the rotator muscles of the spine.

Starting Position: Sit in a straight back chair with the hips pushed back as far as possible, keep the legs parallel to each other and about three to four inches apart and the feet flat on the floor. Maintain this position throughout the movement.

Movements: Reach the left arm around behind the body and grasp the right side frame of the chair back. Rotate the trunk, chest, and head to the left as far as possible. While holding the chair with the right hand, release the left hand and place the thumb and index finger along the base of the right side of the chin on the right. Keep elbow in a horizontal position. Apply a slight pressure with the hand until a very slight stretch pain is felt through the neck and entire back. Hold from three to five seconds. Alternate to each side.

Progression: Do the exercise three times each exercise period.

Precautions: Maintain the hips as described in the starting position. Do not lift or rotate the hips or legs during the stretch.

Exercise 7

Purpose: To stretch the rotator muscles of the lower back and ligaments of the pelvic girdle.

Starting Position: Lie on the back with the arms at side.

Movement: Extend one leg vertically to an angle of 90 degrees. Let the leg hang inward until a slight stretch pain is felt in the lower back. Maintain this position five seconds and return to starting position.

Progression: Do the exercise three times each exercise period.

Precautions: Keep the knees straight and the legs extended throughout the movement. Do not raise the trunk off the mat.

Exercise 8

Purpose: To stretch the rotator muscles of the lower back and the ligaments of the pelvic girdle.

Starting Position: Lie on the back with the arms at shoulder level.

Movement: Raise one leg to a vertical position, keeping the knee extended. The opposite leg should be flat on the floor and in an extended position. Keep the shoulders, arms, and back on the mat. Reach toward the opposite hand with raised leg. Stretch until a stretch pain is felt. Hold three to five seconds and return to starting position.

Progression: Do the exercise three times with each leg each exercise period.

Precautions: Keep the knees straight and the legs extended throughout the movement. Do not raise the trunk off the mat.

Exercise 9

Purpose: To stretch the hip flexor muscles.
Starting Position: Lie on the back.
Movement: Bring the right knee to the chest until a stretch pain is felt. Hold position five seconds and return to starting position.

Progression: Do the exercise five times with each leg each exercise period.

Precautions: Keep extended leg straight. Do not use a bobbing motion.

Exercise 10

Purpose: To stretch the low back muscles and the sacroiliac ligaments.

Starting Position: Lie on the back.

Movements: Bring the knees to the chest and grasp legs just below the knee. Pull the knees toward the axilla keeping the trunk on the mat. Hold the position five seconds and return to the starting position.

Progression: Do the exercise five times and increase one time every other day until 25.

Precautions: Be sure the knees are brought out toward the axilla and not straight to the chest. Do not use a bobbing motion.

Exercise 11

Purpose: To stretch the hip flexor muscles.

Starting Position: Lie on the back on a table with the buttocks at the edge of the table.

Movement: Bring the right leg to the chest and grasp it with laced fingers just below the knee. Let the opposite leg hang freely over the edge of the table. Hold the position until stretch pain is felt and then hold the position for an additional 10 seconds.

Progression: Do the exercise alternately three times to each side and increase one time each side each exercise period until ten.

Precaution: Be sure the leg hangs freely over the edge of the table. Completely relax to ensure stretch. Be sure the knees are brought out toward the axilla and not straight to the chest. Do not use a bobbing motion and stretch only one leg at a time.

Exercise 12

Purpose: To stretch the dorsolumbar spine, the lumbar spine, the lumbosacral area, and the ligaments of the pelvis and hip.

Starting Position: Stand with heels and toes together about 18 inches from and sidewise to a wall. Place one elbow against the wall at shoulder level, with the forearm and hand resting on the wall. The heel of the opposite hand is placed on the upper position of the buttocks. The shoulders are kept in line with the elbow and perpendicular to the wall. Do not allow the shoulders to shift forward. Keep the knees completely extended.

Movement: Contract the abdominal and gluteal muscles strongly while shifting the hips slightly forward and inward toward the wall. This movement is aided by pressure on the buttocks with the heel of the hand.

Progression: Do the exercise three times to each side each exercise period.

Precautions: Keep the knees straight and the body in alignment. Push forward and toward the wall.

Exercise 13

Purpose: To stretch the anterior chest muscles.

Starting Position: Stand facing a corner or a door frame.

Movement: Walk through the door or into the corner. Place hands on the wall or door frame at shoulder level. Keeping the body in good alignment, walk until a stretch pain is felt. Hold the position three to five seconds.

Progression: Do the exercise three times and increase one time every other exercise period until five.

Precautions: Keep the body in good standing posture throughout. *NOTE:* Exercise should also be done with the arms extended 45 degrees upward.

Exercise 14

Purpose: To stretch the spinal ligaments and back muscles.

Starting Position: Hang from stall bars or other apparatus. Grasp the stall bars with the palms forward and the back to the stall bars.

Movement: Hang and maintain this position to tolerance.

Progression: Do the exercise three times daily.

Precautions: Lower the body weight by placing the feet on the stall bar and rest in this position between repetitions.

Exercise 15

Purpose: To stretch the heel cords.

Starting Position: Stand and face the stall bars or wall approximately an arm's length from the wall with the knees straight. Keep the feet three to four inches apart and flat on the floor and the body in alignment.

Movement: Lean forward, catching the body weight with the hands. Keep the head, shoulders, hips, chest, and ankles in alignment. Bend the elbow slowly until stretch pain is felt behind the knees and in the calf of the leg. Hold three to five seconds and return to the starting position.

Progression: Do the exercise three times to start and increase one time each week until five.

Precautions: Keep the leg straight and the heels on the floor. Do not bend at the hips or knees.

Exercise 16

Purpose: To stretch the low back muscles and the sacroiliac ligaments.

Starting Position: Sit in a chair with the hips back in the chair, the feet flat on the floor and parallel to each other.

Movement: Interlock the arms and bend forward from the waist. Keep the hips in the chair at all times. Curl the head, shoulders, and back toward the floor, with the knees spread apart so that the interlocked arms will pass between the knees. Bend forward until a stretch pain is felt in the lower back. Hold the position three to five seconds and then return to the starting position.

Progression: Do the exercise five times and increase two times each exercise period until 25.

Precautions: Keep the hips well back in the seat of the chair at all times. Keep the feet flat on the floor and parallel to each other.

Exercise 17

Purpose: To stretch solaus (back of lower leg) muscle.

Starting Position: Stand and face the wall or doorway approximately 24 inches away from it. Lean forward until the hands rest on the stall bars or wall. Keep the heels on the floor.

Movement: Cross the right lower leg over the left calf at about midcalf level. Bend the knee approximately 15 degrees. Lean forward until a stretch pain is felt in the calf of the leg. Hold the position five seconds. Return to the starting position.

Progression: Do the exercise three times and increase one time every other day until five.

Precautions: Keep the trunk, pelvis, and feet in proper alignment throughout movement. Keep the heels on floor. Do not bend the knee of the weight-bearing leg. Do not arch the back or tilt the pelvis.

General Weight Training Program

Exercise	Equipment	Pounds	Sets	Reps.
Sit up	Weight	5	1	10
Arm Curl	Barbell	1/3 Body Weight	1	6 to 12
Military Press	Barbell	1/2 Body Weight	1	6 to 12
Bent Leg Dead Lift	Barbell	1/2 Body Weight	1	6 to 12
Pull-over and Bench Press	Barbell	1/3 Body Weight	1	6 to 12
Half Squat	Barbell	1/2 Body Weight	1	6 to 12
Stiff Leg Dead Lift	Barbell	1/3 Body Weight	1	6 to 12
Toe Raise	Barbell	1/3 Body Weight	1	6 to 12
Bent Over Row	Barbell	1/3 Body Weight	1	6 to 12
Side-to-Side Bend	Barbell	1/4 Body Weight	1	6 to 12
Leg Curl	Iron Shoe	None	1	20
Neck Isometrics	Partner	Stationary Resistance	1	10 (Hold for 6 sec.)

Weight training, too, can be effective for adult players when dovetailed with a functional program to improve and maintain cardio-pulmonary conditioning. The body responds to a weight training program by increasing strength, endurance and power.

Hoover, who has worked with athletes in virtually all sports, both college and professional, suggests a program for soccer players that can fit in nicely with the heavy running they do.

The resistance, sets, and repetitions indicated for each exercise are intended as beginning goals. The pounds column states the total weight the exerciser should strive to lift. When the beginning goals are met, the exerciser should increase the resistance and decrease the repetitions.

MAINTENANCE OF CONDITIONING (TONING)

1st Week's Work (Daily)

1-440 yard lap (walk, trot, stride)
2-100 yard strides (½ speed)
4-500 yard dashes (speed) without force
1-440 yard trot
10 push-ups
6 Chin-ups
10 Sit-ups
10 Horizontal run (on all fours, stretching the groin muscles)
5 Minutes rope skipping
Jogging until pleasingly tired

2nd Week's Work (Daily)

2-laps and repeat (walk, trot, stride)
3-100 yard strides (½ speed)
6-50 yard dashes (speed) without force
880 yard trot
15 Push-ups
8 Chin-ups
15 Sit-ups
15 Horizontal runs
10 Minutes rope skipping
Jogging until pleasingly tired

3rd Week's Work (Daily)

2-laps (walk, trot, stride)
4-100 yard strides
8-50 yard dashes (speed) without force
1-660 yard trot
20 Push-ups
20 Sit-ups
10 Chin-ups
15 Horizontal runs
10 Minutes rope skipping
Jogging until pleasingly tired

4th Week's Work (Daily)

1-660 yard (walk, trot, stride)
6-100 yard strides (½ speed)
10-50 yard dashes (speed) without force
1-run (6 minutes)
30 Push-ups
40 Sit-ups
10 Chin-ups
20 Horizontal runs
15 Minutes rope skipping
Jogging until pleasingly tired

Weight training should *not* stop when the season begins. It has been shown in a number of experiences that strength levels which were attained in pre-season were lost halfway through the season. It would be wise to have your team do some weight training (two days a week if your team practices five times a week) throughout the season. You will be able to field a strong, more efficient team and one less subject to injury.

The following calisthenics can be used as a warmup for practices or games. It is important for players to stretch their entire body each day so that their suppleness will be retained.

In addition to the exercises listed, remember that rope skipping is one of the finest exercise forms known for increasing coordination, agility, balance, and endurance.

WARM-UP ROUTINE

1. *Body Circling*

The feet are astride with arms upward and straight. The hands are reverse clasped. The legs are straight. Touch the floor outside the left foot, between your feet and then outside the right foot. Circle bend backwards as far as possible. Do ten circles each direction.

2. *Bend and Reach*

The feet are astride with the hands on the hips. Arch back, then bend forward and reach between legs as far as possible with the hands reversed clasped. Do ten repetitions.

3. *High Kicking*

Kick left leg high to right hand. Rise up on toes of right leg. Reverse procedure. Kick ten times each side.

4. *Lateral Pull*

Grasp right elbow with left hand and left elbow with right hand. Hold over head and lean to each side. Repeat ten times to each side.

5. *Twist and Pull*

Adjust arms at shoulder height, twist at waist and pull backward. Repeat ten times in each direction.

6. *Quad Stretch*

While lying on stomach with the legs extended, slowly flex the knee toward the buttocks. Reach back with the left hand, grasp ankle and pull heel down to touch buttocks. Repeat with right side. Do ten repetitions alternately on each leg.

7. *Hamstring Stretch*

Squat down with arms between legs and palms of hands flat on the floor. Raise buttocks up so the legs are straight while palms of hands remain on floor. Hold this position for six seconds. Do ten repetitions of this stretch.

8. *Spread Eagle*

In a sitting position, spread the legs as far as possible and grasp the ankles. Keep ankles straight and touch forehead to the ground. Hold this position for six seconds. Relax and repeat. Do ten repetitions of this stretch.

The soccer coach should give some thought to warming down his players after practice and games just as most coaches warm up players before beginning practice sessions or games, suggests Hoover.

There have been many studies performed to measure effect on performance, if any, of warmup prior to activity. There has been about a 50-50 split between positive results and no effect. Warmup is important, of course, in the prevention of muscular injuries and definitely should

be used as a preparation to vigorous muscular activity. Stimulation of the circulatory system and stretching the muscles involved should be emphasized.

But Hoover believes that the immediate cessation of activity after practices or games is improper and could be harmful.

"I believe all athletes should take the example of many distance runners who, following their race, continue to jog or walk for a significant period of time to cool their bodies down," says Hoover. "Since so much time is spent warming the body up and preparing it for activity, does it not seem logical that some time be utilized to slow it down and return it to normal?"

Hoover feels that a light program of stretching the muscles after practices and games would produce the following results.

1. Restore full range of motion to the muscle.
2. Relax the muscle.
3. Promote normal blood flow which will result in more efficient removal of waste products and restoration of lost nutrients.

With the ever-increasing popularity of the sport, the soccer coach has become a year-round entity. He's not restricted to the playing season alone. The good coach, when not actually coaching, is preparing to coach.

The soccer player, too, is thinking on year-round terms now and it is important that you continue your relationship with him during the off-season.

One way to keep in touch is an off-season conditioning program that will enable him to keep in shape and will keep in mind a goal of being a more valuable player on an even better team in the forthcoming year.

A sample conditioning program follows:

OFF-SEASON CONDITIONING

Warmup Exercises	Duration of Exercise
1. *Head twister*—count 1—bend head forward; count 2—bend head right; count 3—bend head back; count 4—bend head left.	10 reps.

2. *Arm circles*—circle ten times forward and ten times backward.   10 reps.

3. *Trunk roll*—count 1—bend forward; count 2—bend right; count 3—bend back; count 4—bend left.   10 reps.

4. *Shoulder stretch*—grasp hands with arms extended overhead; stretch as far as possible toward the ceiling and hold.   60 secs.

5. *Hamstring stretch*—sit-up position, grab toes and straighten legs; hold   60 secs.

6. *Gastrocnemius (calf) stretch*—stand facing wall four feet away, feet flat on floor, lean forward placing palms against wall, and hold.   60 secs.

7. *Side straddle hop (jumping jacks)*   25 reps.

8. *Running (easy job)*—it is suggested that a figure-8 course of 30–40 yds. be followed to strengthen ankles, legs, and knees.   5 mins.

Conditioning Exercises

These exercises are a combination of calisthenics, isotonics (weighted ball), and isometrics (exercises 7, 8, 9, 10). It is suggested that exercises 1 through 11 be performed three times.

1. *Rope jumping*   5 mins.

2. *Half knee squats*—hands on hips, bend knees half way, return.   25 reps.

3. *Squat thrusts*—count 1—bend knee to full squat; hands on floor outside of legs; count 2—extend legs backward to push-up position; count 3—return to squat; count 4—stand.   25 reps.

4. *Sit-ups*—knee bent and hands behind head.   25 reps.

5. *Leg raises*—lift, spread legs apart, bring together and flutter them up and down, relax.   25 reps.

6. *Pick-ups*—with partner or off wall, field ground balls that are thrown to your left and right.   25 reps.

7. *Finger pull (isometric)*—interlock the first fingers of each hand and pull away from each other for 10 seconds. Do this with each finger, respectively, then with entire hand.   10 secs. each

8. *Finger push (isometric)*—press the first fingers of each hand together and push against each other for 10 seconds. Do this with each finger, respectively, and then with the entire hand.   10 secs. each

9. *Lateral wall pull (isometric)*—with your right side against wall extend your right arm over your head and your palm flat against the wall; push as hard as you can go for 10 seconds. Then do same with left arm.   10 secs. each arm

10. *Lateral wall push (isometric)*—with your right side against the wall and your right arm down at your side and back of your hand against the wall, push out hard to ten seconds. Then do the same with left arm.   10 secs. each arm

11. *Hanging*—hang for 45 seconds with both hands and then 15 seconds with only your throwing arm.   60 secs.

12. *Weighted ball exercises*—if you do not have a weighted ball, you can substitute a 3–5 pound weight.

13. *Throwing*—easy at first, increase velocity and duration weekly.   5 mins.

14. *Sprints*—straight line of 30–40 yards.   10 sprints

NUTRITION

A final word on conditioning. Diet. This is last, but certainly not least, in importance to the well-being of your player. Talk to your players about nutrition.

The regularity of meals is extremely important. Today many people are skipping breakfast and that is a mistake for the athlete. To establish meal habits on a regulated basis of breakfast, lunch and dinner is of equal importance to the types of foods eaten. Rushing through meals or skipping meals can be very detrimental.

Nutrition is the science of properly nourishing the body—providing for its growth, maintenance and repair. Foods are broken into five basic food groups:

1. grain products
2. fats and sugars
3. meats, poultry, fish, eggs, legumes and nuts
4. milk and milk products
5. vegetables and fruits

A balanced diet includes foods from these groups every day. Vitamins are present in all natural foods: fruits, vegetables, grains and animal and plant fats. With a well-balanced diet, supplementary vitamins will be unnecessary.

Fluid replacement during practice and games is most important. This is especially true during hot days or particularly demanding practice sessions.

Convince your players that these conditioning programs will be only as effective as they make them and that it is vitally important to the team that each and every player keep himself fit. If a player consistently abuses his body away from the practice field, no amount of exercise will keep him in tip-top shape for the non-stop running and thinking he must do on the field.

6

You and Your Goalkeeper: Techniques for Tending Goal

The goalkeeper needs to be a special kind of kid who is able to concentrate and to tolerate the extremes of going flaky from boredom and slaphappy from getting shot at. Goalkeepers are to be loved not yelled at.

Lou Confessore, Coach

The goalkeeper is the man who bars the door, using his hands and every ounce of sinew and bone as the latch.

A good goalkeeper is absolutely essential to a winning team. When he is playing at the top of his game, he raises the game of the players in front of him. If he plays badly the team will probably lose regardless of how your other players perform.

He's a rare combination of eiderdown and steel. The way you handle him is a key to your success as a winning coach. As important as the development of a goalkeeper's physical skills is his mental toughness. The goalkeeper never really wins. He only does what he's supposed to do . . . or loses.

Tell a goalkeeper he tends goal like the ancient mariner who "stoppeth one of three," and you have lost him forever. There is the old goalkeeper's gag that "he was so fed up he tried to commit suicide by throwing himself in front of a bus—but it passed under his body!"

Hearing stories like these is enough to make the prospective goalkeeper switch to another position . . . or another sport.

Goalkeeping is an unnatural way of life in the most natural of team sports. It's like riding a roller coaster.

Once you find a player who accepts this and can turn his attention to developing the unique conditioning and skill techniques of patrolling his area, you've found your man.

45

The goalkeeper is a specialist and, except at the very young levels, he requires different coaching and training than the other players.

More is expected of a soccer goalkeeper than his counterpart in any other sport. His responsibility is defending an upright, open area eight feet high and eight yards across. His battleground is the 6-by-24-yard box in front of the goal—any ball that invades that area should be his. He should have control over an even larger territory—the 18-by-44-yard box that is the penalty area. He can put hands on the ball anywhere within this larger area and a good goalkeeper will not be afraid to venture out into this wide expanse.

Naturally, he is the last man responsible for keeping the ball out of the net. He should also be the director of the defense and must establish rapport and means of communication with his fullback teammates.

Not only is the goalkeeper important to your team in this obvious role as a stopper of balls aimed at the goal, but as a starter on attack as well. A coach's best-laid offensive plans work best at midfield, not when the ball is bounding around in front of his own team's goalmouth.

Finding the proper player to tend goal is not always easy. At the youth level, it is best to give the opportunity to any player who wishes it. Never *force* a youngster into the position of goalkeeper. Experiment. You might be fortunate enough to find a natural for the position. If not, you must spend sufficient time to develop your finest prospect.

You will need a good athlete, preferably one with good height and good hands. He must have courage. He will be blocked, elbowed, and bumped. He will crash heavily to the ground, often in the path of oncoming players with goals lighting up their eyes. He must be prepared to

Shep Messing frustrates another scoring opportunity with aggressive save.

play with pain and find himself again and again about the goal.

He must have quick reflexes. And he must work hard to keep these reflexes sharp. Agility is vital for quick adjustments on balls that are deflected and kicked, headed, or kneed goalward.

A goalkeeper should be cocky. He should want the ball shot at him and should be the field general for the defense, yelling instructions to his fullbacks, directing play in the goal area when the opposing team is attacking and during his team's clearing procedures. He should have a thorough knowledge of the duties and capabilities of each of his teammates and the ability to see, describe, and counter offensive and defensive patterns as they develop in front of him.

Finding one player with all these necessary attributes will be tough enough, but you should also have a dependable backup tender. An injury to or unexpected absence of your regular goalkeeper can leave you in a vexing situation.

You will also find that two goalkeepers can work together to keep their reflexes sharp and, of course, the competition for the job will make your number one man put forth more effort.

Unless you can afford the luxury of an assistant coach or possess a goalkeeping specialist to work with your goalkeepers, it will be difficult for you to give worthwhile instructional attention to this sensitive cog in your team.

But you must find a way.

The first and most important concentration of your goalkeeper should be catching the ball.

There is no rule in any sport older than "Keep your eye on the ball." This dictum should be especially impressed upon the goalkeeper, for he must watch the ball into his hands no matter what chaos is occurring around him.

The hands should be behind the ball, so that the thumbs are almost touching. The wider apart the hands, the better chance the ball has to slip through. The hands and arms should be relaxed, so that the ball can be gathered in to the body. The goalkeeper should keep his body behind the ball whenever possible and bring the ball into the body after the catch to reduce the chances of its being knocked away from him.

On diving and leaping plays, of course, he will not have that body backup, so you cannot over-emphasize the fact that his hands, wrists and arms should be flexible and that the catch of the ball is first and foremost. He will develop the knack of bringing the ball to his chest for protection with increased speed as he handles many catches.

When diving for balls, the goalkeeper should face the ball and launch his body sideways, so that he will land on his hip and the back of his shoulder. This will prevent injury and also enable him to bring the ball more quickly to his box. It is important that he secure the ball. A deflection is almost a sure goal, since the goalkeeper is down.

Punching the ball away should occur only when the keeper feels he cannot control the ball by catching it. Punching is dangerous, because it increases the odds on the opponent regaining possession, but sometimes it is a necessity, especially when the goalkeeper is off balance or already has stretched as far as he can and feels he cannot secure it.

The punch is executed with the full fist or both fists. Often the punch will have to be made in heavy traffic, so he should bring one knee up in front of his body for both leverage and protection when leaping. Punching the ball is especially effective on crosses and corner kicks, because that is a time when the goal area is crowded with players from both teams.

A goalkeeper should not be afraid to move forward to pick off crosses or cut the angle on an advancing forward, but once he makes the decision to come out he must not dilly-dally or harbor second thoughts. He should advance aggressively, calling teammates off the ball.

When making the decision to leave his goal, he should make sure the odds of reaching the ball before a defender favor him. He should not vacate his post for a 50-50 ball that could result in a deflection and a scoring opportunity for the opponent.

Moving quickly and aggressively is especially important when the goalkeeper leaves the goal to narrow the shooting angle for an advancing forward. If the goalie moves slowly, the man with the ball has many options: he can lob the ball over the goalie's head, he can feint and dribble around the goalie for a shot or he can make a square pass to a teammate for a shot at

Leaping ability
by goalkeepers is important,
but good hands are vital.

the open goal. By moving swiftly, the goalkeeper reduces those options, may befuddle the man with the ball and often can smother the ball before the attacker can get off a shot.

On corner kicks, the goalkeeper should position himself closer to the far post so he can move forward or out to catch the cross.

When his team is setting up a wall against free kicks, the goalkeeper should move to the near post to line up the end player on the wall, then take up his position for the kick on the other side of the goal. This gives him full vision of the kick and he is prepared to move across the goal to intercept a ball chipped over the wall.

Unfortunately, the goalkeeper must deal with another type of free kick, the penalty kick. It's the goalie versus the kicker, one on one, 12 yards apart. Gunfight at OK Corral, the odds stacked heavily for the guy in the black hat. A recent North American Soccer League study

revealed the kicker is successful on about 85 percent of the kicks.

You will hear even experienced goalkeepers claim there is little the goalie can do except guess which way to dive and accept the 50-50 chance it's the right direction.

As a coach who wants to win, don't send your goalkeeper out there to face the situation with so little faith. Give him some ammunition. Spend some practice time on penalty kicking. It will not only aid the player or players who will be kicking penalties for your team, but give your goalkeeper an opportunity to size up the situation. Discuss with him a standard operating procedure for improving the odds, even if only a little.

1. Stall. Make the kicker wait. Stroll to the side of the goal while the referee is clearing the goal area and let the kicker ponder his situation. Think of yourself as a batter stepping out of the box to break a pitcher's rhythm.

2. As you take your position on the line (the goalkeeper cannot move his feet until the ball is kicked), study the kicker's angle of approach. This may tip off the direction of the kick.

3. Keep your balance until the last possible second. Don't leap too soon. If the kicker alters his approach or fails to get full foot on the ball and chips it, you may still have a chance to react.

4. If the ball is chipped or kicked badly and you're off balance, try to deflect or punch the ball out.

5. If you're able to make contact with the ball, regain your balance as quickly as possible because it may still be in play.

6. If it lands in the back of the net, forget it. You've done your best. Your time will come.

Shep Messing, the well-traveled North American Soccer League goalie, learned at an early age to use his own initiative in combating the dreaded penalty kick. In a qualifying match for the 1972 Olympic Games, the irrepressible Messing was confronted with a penalty kick tie-breaker after the United States had played Costa Rica to a standstill through the regulation game and overtime.

As the first Costa Rican prepared for the first kick, Messing suddenly commenced shrieking newly learned Spanish curse words. The startled kicker blew the shot. With the next kicker poised for his attempt, Shep tore off his shirt and the distracted Latin missed. With Costa Rica needing a goal on its final try to even the tie-breaker count, Messing sprinted to the penalty spot, wrestled the ball from the astonished opponent and threw it aside, then strolled back to set up for the kick. Still muttering about the antics of the crazy gringo, the kicker shot wide

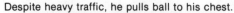

Despite heavy traffic, he pulls ball to his chest.

Goalie soars up for a cross, hands spread wide, thumbs close together.

Goalkeeper's form for distributing ball to fullback to start attack.

and the United States won. Such drastic action isn't recommended. As a matter of fact, he could have been ejected from the game for unsportsmanlike behavior.

But remember to praise your goalkeeper for his efforts, even if he dives the wrong way and misses a penalty shot by a mile. Don't let it ruin his game.

After making a save during regular action, the goalkeeper is permitted four steps before releasing the ball. He may not walk around with the ball, for more than four steps will result in an indirect free kick for the opponent. Your goalkeeper can get around this rule by dropping the ball to the ground after four steps, then collect it again for another four steps.

He must be careful that no opponents are lurking nearby when he drops the ball, however, because it is a free ball. Tony Chursky, of the Seattle Sounders, won't soon forget his lapse in the 1977 North American Soccer League championship game when he put the ball down after a fine save. The Cosmos' Steve Hunt stole from behind Chursky, captured the ball and scored a goal while the humiliated goalkeeper was tackling him into the net.

Distributing the ball is the goalkeeper's next order of business and a particularly important one in his education. He now becomes the ignition key for the attack and if he doesn't perform this duty well, he'll face another barrage from the enemy.

Punting or drop-kicking the ball is the traditional form of clearing and, especially for the beginning goalie, it will seem to be the safest because he will experience a secure feeling with a long, powerful kick that clears the area.

A simple long kick of the ball, however, may result in only temporary relief because he will place pressure on his teammates to capture a 50-50 ball, that is, the opponent has as much chance of gaining possession as his own team.

So he should be able to kick not only for distance, but for accuracy. Vision is important here since a well-placed kick will land in an area occupied by more of his teammates than the opponent. Even if his own team fails to control the ball, it may place the other team in an unworkable field position. The key to good punting is repetition. The basics must be mastered, and once mastered, the goalkeeper should be a slave to them. Variety should come only in the direction of the ball. He should not kick straight down the middle unless he spots open teammates or has a center forward who is particularly good in the air. Otherwise, try one wing, then the other.

By going a step further and varying his methods of distribution, the goalkeeper can keep his opponent completely unsettled on clears. Throwing the ball to a teammate running into open space can trigger the offense in a most effective way.

The goalkeeper can throw the ball overarm (akin to a baseball throw) or underarm (more like bowling), but either way the feet should be spread apart for good body balance. On the overarm throw, because the soccer ball is bigger than a baseball, it should be cupped firmly by the hand and wrist. On the underarm, the same is true because, of course, there are no holes in the soccer ball like in a bowling ball. But the motions are like baseball and bowling and, as in those sports, the follow-through is important for maximum accuracy.

Because the goalkeepers often feel left out of practices unless there is someone assigned to work with them, you should give them a training program which they can conduct on their own. The following program could be used by the goalkeepers in practice as well as in their pre-game warmup.

1. *Individual*
a. 10 push-ups
b. 10 sit-ups
c. 10 roller coasters (lie on stomach, raise arms and legs, and rock)
d. 10 bridges (lie on back, raise body with hands and feet)
2. *With Another Goalkeeper*
a. 10 punts (kick to each other. Concentrate on approach to ball and follow-through)
b. 10 throws (throw to each other. Work on follow-through)
c. 10 rolls (roll to each other)
d. 10 punches (either with other goalkeeper or during team drills)
3. *Team Drill*
   Goalie Pinball—(Goalkeeper in center of group of four or five players, preferably including fullbacks, who have two balls passing into the goalie one at a time to catch and throw or roll back to player without a ball. Goalkeeper should concentrate on clean catch, good return delivery and reaction to next pass. Passes may be on ground or chipped.)

7

Practice, a Flow to Form: How to Plan Training Sessions

Practice . . . because when you don't, somebody, somewhere, is, and when they play you, they will beat you.

Bill Bradley

Organization is a flow to form. Without organization, soccer training can be disorganized hysteria, a yawnfest, or a holocaust of confusion. Sessions can be hard work, draining the physical and mental energies of you and your players. They can all be fun, with nobody learning anything and eventually disintegrating into boredom.

Coaching is the management of players to achieve a common purpose effectively. It begins with practice. This is where you demonstrate the skill to dominate without whipping the initiative out of your players. With control of practice sessions you will be able to carry on an interplay with your players, engaging their skills, abilities, and creativity to work with you and flow to your form.

Obviously, training sessions should be planned so that the time leading up to the first game and each game thereafter can be used diligently and intelligently.

Coaches differ on the methods used to apply their fundamental teaching and game theories. You must be governed by your own instincts on the time allottted for drills as opposed to scrimmage, time devoted to offense or defense, the importance of pointing for a specific opponent, the emphasis placed upon individual and team instruction, how much work and how much fun, or how to merge the two.

For youth players, practice sessions necessarily should be directed toward teaching of fundamentals and principles . . . and fun. For older players, concentration can be shifted to maintenance of conditioning, reviewing fundamentals and development of tactics, perhaps installing new plays for a specific opponent, or adding to the team's repertoire to break up signs of indifference or staleness.

And fun plays a part in practices even at the professional level. There are many games to make practice fun and many pro coaches recommend and employ loose, small-sided scrimmages and other competitive drills to break up the monotony when training becomes too heavy.

Jimmy Gabriel, coach of the Seattle Sounders, says many of his players have told him at the end of a season: "I've enjoyed soccer for the first time since I was a kid when we used to put our jackets down and play for fun."

Gabriel says too many coaches base practice and playing on hard work and physical courage.

"The fun thing in doing anything is showing your ability and your skills," says Gabriel. "If a player is enjoying himself, then you have a good player. It's when a player is not enjoying himself that you have a player who sets a low standard for what his ability should be. I like to bring out the creativity of my players."

Coaches must plan practices in respect to what they wish to accomplish. Goals should be established for each player and the team as a unit each day. A good plan will eliminate interruptions and delays, providing for the amount of work to be finished on time, and sending the players away with an uplifted feeling and eager to return for the next day's workout.

Find a quiet time with pencil and paper to plan a series of practices that will fit the age and experience level of your players. Consider objectives for each player and how you will deal with the players on an individual basis to reach these objectives. Set a time schedule for each day's work. Study ways to divide the team into workable units. Jot down the drills for teaching techniques you will use, each day building to a tactical lesson that will implement the skills practiced that day.

Check your equipment needs. A ball for each player, if possible. If not, at least six or eight balls are needed. Highway marker cones can be used in many ways, including as goals for small-sided games, course markers for dribbling relays, and as position markers for younger teams. A whistle, stop watch, clipboard, and pen are handy items. A small medical kit should always be included in your equipment bag.

If you have an assistant, meet with him and discuss team practice plans, welcoming his input. Discuss his responsibilities. Work out a system for discipline, so that players will not become confused by different standards of behavior expectations from the coaches.

At the first practice, let your players know in no uncertain terms what you expect of them. Plain talk is essential. Make sure they understand what you mean. One youth coach explained to his players that the next practice would be 4 to 6. A 12-year-old winger showed up at four minutes to six o'clock.

You may have the players warm up as a group, but the authors recommend that the players be instructed on the methods of warm-up, which stretching and agility exercises should be used to help prevent pulled muscles and permit them to warm up at their own respective paces. Some players get loose quicker than others. Some coaches set a starting time for practice and expect the players to be warmed up and ready to work at that time.

It is likely you will want the first practice to involve an evaluation of skills so that you can get an idea which players are suited for which positions. You may want to record the times and distances, but even if you don't, these tests will provide you with a good initial appraisal of your players.

A typical evaluation test:

1. Have each player sprint 50 yards for time.
2. Dribbling over 50-yard distance for time.
3. Dribbling through cones over 50-yard distance for time.
4. Kick for distance with each foot.
5. Kick at target (could be open goal or smaller target of cones with each foot).
6. Head thrown balls at target (could be open goal).
7. Pass with inside of each foot at target of cones.
8. Each player serve as goalkeeper for balls kicked into goalmouth at various angles.

This, of course, will not be a conclusive test, but it will give you a starting point and provide a measuring stick for player improvement. And

Tampa Bay's Rodney Marsh doesn't have much chance with Chicago Sting's Karl-Heinz Granitza controlling ball with his body.

you will be able to form some general impressions about the skills each player possesses in relation to the qualities needed for various positions.

Players who show surehandedness and agility, and who reveal a real desire for the job, will warrant further tests as a goalkeeper. You will want to test their ability to concentrate and their courage.

For the defending positions, you'll want to try players who excelled in the distance kicking and heading tests. You'll need to find out if these players can tackle and keep their heads.

Midfield candidates will include those players who are accurate passers, demonstrate good ball sense and good dribbling techniques.

Forward players are those who display the greatest speed, good ability in the air and superior shooting accuracy. The wings need to be fast, good dribblers and possess the ability to cross the ball on the run. Strikers should be quick and mobile and your team's best shooters.

As practices progress, so will players improve their skills and you may change players and positions frequently until you come up with the right combination.

Your system of play will evolve from the players. Systems don't make players, players make systems.

For more experienced players, you may be able to quickly evaluate the skills of the players with a game of one-touch, a regular game in

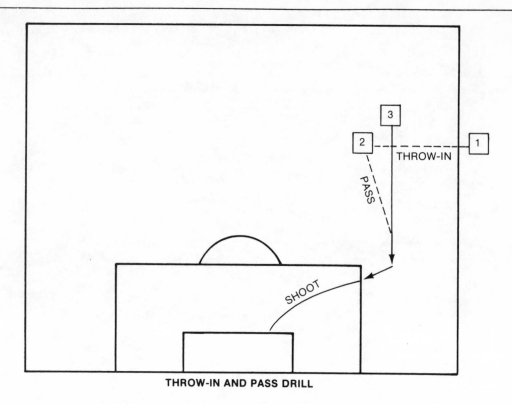

THROW-IN AND PASS DRILL

which the players must play the ball immediately with a pass, head, or shot. This is a
severe first test for the players and even professional players may not respond quickly, but
there will soon be a flow to the game and you
will be able to appraise which players are able
to use other players and which ones are able to
move without the ball. You will see which players are workers and which can read the game.

In fact, one-touch and two-touch are ideal
games to use throughout the season in practice.
They are considered "fun" games by professionals, who often use this technique in short-sided
games (with smaller goals which become very
competitive). To watch the pros move the ball in
such games is to view craftsmen at work, men
who know what is going on around them and
who understand the basis of sound team play.

Non-professionals will not produce the same
results, but these games are marvelous ways to
improve the reactions of your players and to
impress upon them the importance of their
teammates and how to use them.

There are a number of ways to play short-
sided games. You may play them with or without goalkeepers, full or half field (or even
smaller) and with restrictions other than one-
touch and two-touch, such as left or right foot
only, all passes ten yards or more, no goals or
many goals.

It is important that you supervise these games
closely. If it's one-touch, make sure the players
don't try to sneak in an extra touch or two.
Penalize the team for infractions. Establish that
you want all drills executed properly.

Drills on fundamentals should be simple and
you should supervise closely the execution of
skills and correct mistakes on the spot.

A few sample drills for beginners:

1. Instep Passing

Divide players into two parallel lines facing
each other about 15 yards apart with five yards
between players in each line. Players kick with
instep to opposite line with first right foot, then
left foot. Watch for form in passing and trapping return pass. Move lines farther apart for
distance kicking.

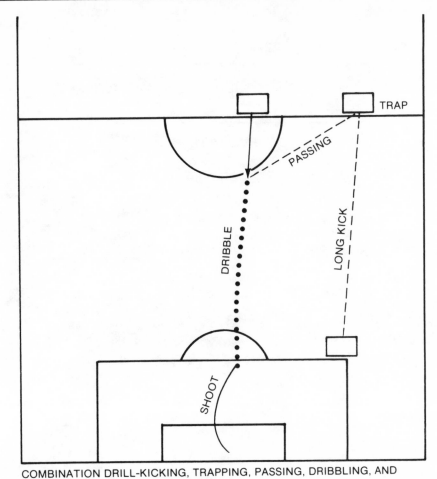

COMBINATION DRILL-KICKING, TRAPPING, PASSING, DRIBBLING, AND SHOOTING

2. Shooting

Form players in two single file lines facing the goal. The first man in line 1 passes ball to the first man in line 2 who shoots at goal on first touch. The shooter retrieves the ball and goes to line 1, the passer goes to line 2. Correct for approach to ball, accuracy of passes and shots.

3. Inside-of-the-foot Passing

Form players in two lines at midfield. First player in line 1 passes to first player in line 2 and they pass to each other to goalline and return. Watch for accurate lead passes and ball control. Later add defensive man who should apply light pressure at first, then mark tighter and try to steal ball.

4. Throw-in and Pass

Form players in three lines near touch line. Player 1 throws to player 2 who volley passes to 3. Add defender to give opposition.

5. Combination (kicking for distance, trapping, passing, dribbling and shooting)

Form players in three lines, 1 at the six yard box, 2 and 3 parallel at midfield, about ten yards apart. Player 1 long kicks to player 2, who traps and feeds lead pass to player 3 who dribbles across line at top of 18-yard box and shoots. To expand on this drill, you may have player 1 move to defend against player 3. This is an effective pre-game warmup drill.

You should have a few drills handy to break

Keeping body between defender and the ball for control.

the monotony of practice if such signs appear. Here are a few "fun" drills:

1. Using Your Head (Thinking man's drill)

Form players in single file line facing you. Tell the first player in line you will throw the ball up. If you yell "Head It," he should catch it with his hands. If you yell "Catch It," he should head it back to you. After each player has had a few chances, tell them to head it when you yell "Head It" and catch it when you yell "Catch It." Young players, especially, will get some laughs from this one without realizing you are learning something about their reactions.

2. Dodge Ball

Players form a circle with one or two players in the center. Using two balls, players in circle try to hit player or players in center by kicking across the circle. Stress form on instep kicking, first time kicking and trapping and quick kicking.

3. Do This, Do That Warmup

Stand before the players as you would for an exercise drill. Execute, slowly at first then faster, a series of simple arm exercises saying "Do This," "Do This." They should follow your arm movements. But when you say "Do That," with one of the movements they should freeze. Player or players who follow your move when you say "Do That" performs five pushups.

4. Dribble Tag

All players formed within a specified area, perhaps the center circle, each with a ball. One player is "It," and the others, all of whom must keep dribbling and moving, try to avoid his tag. If player accidentally allows his ball to leave the circle, he is "It."

5. Soccer Tennis

Played with four or five on a side. Tennis rules apply, except that the service is taken with a half-volley kick, the ball may be played three times before the return, and the ball may bounce only once before being played.

Whether practice time is work or fun is a decision you will make on your players' reaction to the sessions. It is up to the players. A player who refuses to get himself in shape will find practices brutally hard labor, while the ones who have made the personal sacrifices to stay in shape will enjoy whatever is thrown at them.

It should be impressed upon the players that they are expected to execute in practices exactly the way they would in a game. Carelessness in practices will carry over into game situations. How your players perform in practice can make the difference between victory or defeat in games.

The time of your practice is important.

Professional teams normally train in the morning because soccer is the full-time job of all the players. They report to training early enough before a 10 a.m. session to dress and receive treatment or be taped. Breakfasts have been digested and the session will be concluded by noon so that players will be able to enjoy a regular lunchtime.

Non-professionals, including amateur, high school, college and youth teams, usually are able to practice only in the late afternoon and evening. Sometimes this plays havoc with the regularity of meals. Coaches should try, if possible, to schedule workouts close to midafternoon so that lunches will have been digested and the players will be able to eat dinner at a proper time.

Remember to set a theme for each practice. Players need to know they are mastering skills for a reason and that the results of their efforts will be manifested in a game.

You may want to point the practice toward correcting a major team weakness, such as defensive clearing procedures or midfield passing, or concentrating on your attacking plans for an upcoming opponent.

Finally, don't forget to praise the players for their practice efforts. Call them together at the end of the session for a brief talk about what was accomplished, what needs to be improved and a comment about each player's practice performance. Let them know that you have noticed an improvement in kicking with the weak foot or the mastering of a skill that was a long time coming.

It is vital that sessions finish on the upbeat, with the players wanting more.

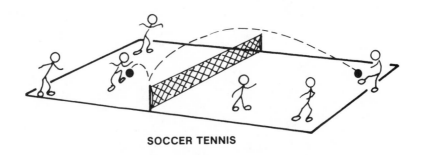

SOCCER TENNIS

8

Building a Winner: Putting Together the Pieces for Victory

Success in solving the problem depends on choosing the right aspect, on attacking the fortress from the accessible side.

—George Polya

Soccer is a game of running and thinking. Not thinking about running. Until now, your players have been doing a lot of running—while learning skills, scrimmaging, getting fit—but little thinking.

In order to persuade your players to think on the field in a way that will produce favorable results, you must be a thinking man, too. Think constructively, but seek independence. Constructive thinking is disciplined thinking, but don't conform to an established pattern simply because it has always been followed. Soccer is a creative game and it needs creative coaches as well as creative players. Stale, old-fashioned

thinking is one of the major reasons the game of soccer has taken so long to emerge as a major force in the United States.

After you have sorted out your best players, it is time to build a defense and install an offense. A system of play. We have said systems fit the players, not vice-versa, and it is the players, not systems, who will win games. You must provide them with the tools to achieve success.

The player, then, is the essence. It is your job as an intelligent, thinking coach to develop a system that will weld together player skills and positional functions in a manner that will exploit strengths and minimize weaknesses.

There are any number of ways to align your players. The easiest way to look at the formation is in terms of three rows—defenders, midfielders and forwards—backed up, of course, by the goalkeeper. The system most popular now is the 4-3-3 which offers numerical defensive sta-

A difficult view of the game. Not a good technique.

bility with four fullbacks, three midfielders and three forwards.

The attack must be coordinated with the defense—each must be able to change to the other with speed and fluidity. The alignment must afford defensive balance, yet permit the immediate development of attacking measures.

Momentum, the ghost who walks in all sports, becomes your Holy Grail, and your chances of capturing this intangible and elusive force lie with your defense. Defenses are better able to sustain momentum than offenses. Your team will score goals with an outstanding attack, but won't *win* without defense.

There is no time too early in your relationship with your players to impress them with defensive importance. Be a stickler for good defensive

play. You'll find offensive principles easier to teach as defensive fundamentals become more ingrained in your players.

The key in the 4-3-3 is the midfield line, the engine room of the team, a veritable pendulum swinging back and forth. On offense, the midfielders move forward; when the ball is lost, they immediately start thinking defense.

Midfielders are the personification of the running and thinking philosophy. They need stamina and brains. Speed is helpful at these positions, but work rate is more important.

All midfielders should excel at controlling the ball, be able to turn with the ball, and kick it with authority. They should be able to distribute the ball with short passes or long, accurate passes to the wings. They must have good vision and awareness for they often will be working in heavy traffic and must find space to operate.

Shooting ability can be an asset, but in the three-man midfield, one player should excel on defense. His defensive skills will make this midfielder vitally important to the team effort.

He is called upon to jam up an enemy attack in its early stages, collect the ball and move to space to hit a teammate with a pass to trigger his own team's offense. Midfield control is all-important and the man in the center is the key to it. His area of responsibility ranges from the top of both penalty boxes and territory laterally as well in backing up the midfielders to his right and left.

In initiating the attack, your center midfielder must have good vision and awareness as well as a cool head. He must not try to play dangerous balls forward with only a hope and prayer that something will happen.

The outside midfielders do just as much running, but their responsibilities may differ according to their individual capabilities and your game plan. It is important that these midfielders

do a lot of running when they don't have the ball. They take themselves out of the game when they stop moving and looking for space to run into. They are basically support players on the attack, but may find themselves overlapping the wing on a passing exchange or cutting inside to fire a shot from the top of the penalty box. They must be prepared to defend as soon as the opponent gains possession. Many times possession can be regained immediately after losing it by the alertness of a midfielder.

The right and left midfielders often are the takers of free kicks and the throwers on throw-ins. They should be prepared to make the most of these re-starts. A study has revealed that 40 percent of goals scored in modern soccer result from set plays.

The coach should endeavor to spend sufficient practice time applied to game situations on these re-starts so that every player knows his responsibility.

Quick kicking sometimes can gain a numerical advantage, but it will not benefit your team if the kicker and his teammates are not on the

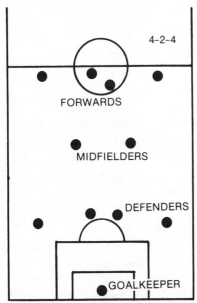

THE 4-2-4 PROVIDES OFFENSIVE STRENGTH; FULLBACKS PUSH FORWARD AS WING ATTACKERS IN THIS FORMATION

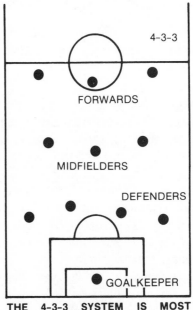

THE 4-3-3 SYSTEM IS MOST POPULAR NOW BEING USED

Running with the ball and without it. Note dribbler's teammate moving into supporting position.

same wave-length. When the opponent builds a "wall" (line of defenders which must be ten yards from the ball), there are ways to beat it with plenty of practice and quick-thinking.

One way to beat the wall is to chip the ball over or curve it around. The Chicago Sting's Karl-Heinz Granitza is especially adept at curving the ball past a defensive wall with the outside-of-the-foot kick and he has scored numerous goals by that method.

There are many variations of set plays for free kicks and an imaginative coach will be able to create his own. Working on such plays in practice also is interesting for the players. One such play can be used when you receive a free kick

and the opponent sets up a wall on one side of the penalty box. Your center midfielder approaches the ball as if to shoot, but runs on past the ball. The outside midfielder, who has started running at the same time, passes the ball to the center forward for a shot on goal. Three other players will be moving toward the goal, too, for diversion and to be in position for a rebound.

Throw-ins, too, should be taken quickly to gain an advantage. Player movement to create space is important as is the understanding by each player of his role for the throw-in. The thrower is usually unmarked at a throw-in and he should move quickly onto the field and head for space after taking the throw-in. Potential

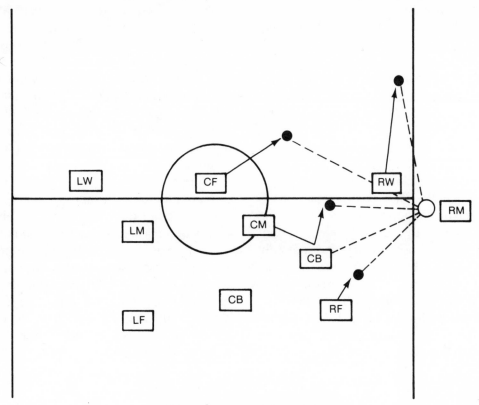

POSSIBLE RECEIVERS OF THROW-IN

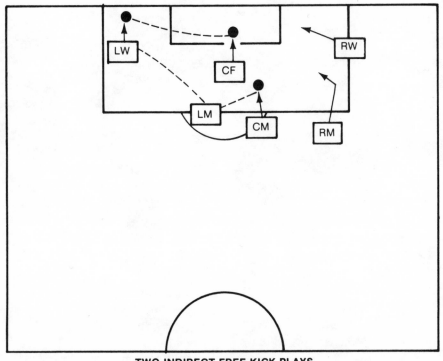

TWO INDIRECT FREE KICK PLAYS

receivers should not crowd the thrower—it is easier to move into the throw-in than away from it.

Behind the midfielders are the defenders. With the four-man line, there are two fullbacks, the outside men, and two central defenders, often with specialized duties as stopper and sweeper.

It is important that the two men in the middle be strong, courageous and good in the air. The outside defenders need not be as strong physically and it is beneficial if they are fast and have good ball control. A good fullback should be able to keep pace with the wings, since he will be marking the opposing wing and possibly overlapping his own wing as an extra attacker with the ball. Chicago Sting Captain Bruce Wilson, a left fullback who has been named to the North American Soccer League all-star team three years running, assisted on ten goals in 1977 while with the Vancouver Whitecaps. Wilson's forte is playing a wall pass at midfield, taking the ball down the wing and crossing it.

All four defenders should be outstanding tacklers and it should be stressed to them that they should stay on their feet as much as possible. The sliding tackle is great entertainment, but the chances of winning the ball should be weighed because when the fullback is down and out of the game, he's not much help to his teammates.

There are two types of defensive play—man-to-man and zone. In man-to-man the defensive man marks an opposing player. In the zone, he covers an area. Many teams use a combination, marking man for man in and around the penalty box and using zone coverage up field. Another form of the combination exists when a fullback is marking the wing man for man on his side, but when the ball is on the other wing, he moves to cover in the middle of the field, thereby cutting off the path of onrushing

Marking the dribbler—note defender's balance.

Veteran pro Gerry Ingram prepares to turn with ball and beat opponent.

attackers and adding depth to the defense between the ball and the goal.

Another way to stop the opponents' attack is with an offside plan, your fullbacks suddenly moving forward when the ball is about to be passed by the opponent toward the goal, placing the advancing attackers in offside positions.

The offside plan is dangerous to use unless your players thoroughly understand. An intelligent attack won't fall for it, in fact may take advantage for an easy scoring opportunity.

The four-fullback system provides man to man coverage with the outside fullbacks marking the wings and the center back (stopper) covering the center forward and an extra man, the sweeper, who operates behind to provide cover for all the players, particularly the fullbacks. When a man is beaten, the sweeper should pick up an opponent who is free since other teammates will have been called upon to engage the man with the ball.

The sweeper also provides more security for the fullbacks who are converting defense into attack. Rather than booming the ball out of danger with a long kick into heavy traffic at centerfield, the fullback can gain a little more time to serve the ball more accurately to a forward.

Fullbacks, like other players, should be taught to move after passing the ball to enable teammates to return the ball to them or to make decoy runs to provide space for other players.

For fullbacks, the danger area is the last third of the field, outside the penalty area. This is when marking must be tight and tackles must be made.

When discussing defense with your team, impress each player with the thought that he, as an individual, and the team as a whole should try to dominate the opponent, to win every ball that's free, and to control the ball as much as possible.

Impress them with the importance of defensive talking to teammates. This not only will help strategically in making sure each man is marking the right opponent on switches, but will help keep a team aggressive.

In the forward line, you must have players who have the skill to beat a defender. Center forwards, often called strikers, and wings alike must have the capability to take the ball past opponents.

Although many coaches like to have a big man who is good in the air at the center forward position, strikers come in all shapes and sizes. The Sting's sensational German striker, Karl-Heinz Granitza, who has averaged a goal· per game in the North American Soccer League, is a big bruiser who isn't particularly good in the air, but possesses marvelous control of the ball in heavy traffic, excellent screening ability and a powerful shot with either foot.

On the other hand, a former Sting player, John Kowalik, one of the North American Soccer League's all-time leading scorers, was a fragile-looking little fellow who scuttled around the penalty area with the intense urgency of a squirrel. Ironically, Kowalik possessed excellent ability in the air for his size.

Granitza and Kowalik, for all their differences in size and ability, have one thing in common—they score goals.

Perhaps the most exciting players to coach are the wingers, who should have speed and good technique. Short, sharp bursts of speed and the ability to beat a man in the open field are most important.

The first thing forwards must learn is that what they do without the ball is essential to the team. They must be able to find and use space and this calls for a lot of running. It also calls for unselfishness and sacrifice, for most of the running will be unproductive for the individual but invaluable to the team.

They do not have to be strong defensively, but the team benefits tremendously if the striker and wings will harass the opponents' clearing procedures. When possession is lost, the forwards should immediately look for areas in front of opponents to obstruct angles of passing.

We will reiterate that your pattern of offense must fit the abilities of your players, so it is probable that your starting point will come after watching your team scrimmage, and seeing what tendencies they have. You'll learn whether you can use quick-break principles or close ball control. It will soon be evident if they prefer give and go tactics. Playing balls forward in the air or on the ground must be dictated by your personnel.

It is unwise to allow your players to dictate to you the kind of offense they *want* to use. It must be your decision, based on the tendencies they show.

The wings and striker have key parts in most re-starts. On the throw-in, the striker may position himself to receive the throw and the wing may line up in a close position and sprint down the touch line for a throw. If the ball goes to the striker and he is closely marked, he may play the ball back to the thrower. There are many variations of set plays from throw-ins, but they must be practiced repeatedly to get the timing exact.

On corner kicks, usually a specialty of the wings, there are also variations that should be practiced so that every man knows his role. Many teams prefer a short, hard kick to the near corner for the forward on the near post to ram home or to knock across to the far post. Some wings will boom the ball high across the goal area for the other wing to head or kick home. It is important that the off wing not be pulled too far inside the goal area so that he will have to chase a ball that clears the pack in front of the goal. He should be attacking the far post facing the goal.

For a particular opponent, you may want to change your alignment to exploit a weakness or counter a strength by moving one of the forwards into the midfield for better midfield control, moving a midfielder into the front line for more attacking strength or even playing a three-man line of defenders without a sweeper.

Whatever your plan of attack, it all boils down to one objective: Put the ball in the back of the net!

9

What Hath the Coach Wrought? How to Get the Most Out of Your Talent

If you can meet with Triumph and Disaster
And treat those two imposters just the same.

—Rudyard Kipling

Winning isn't everything, but wanting to win is.

—Vince Lombardi

I love winners who cry and losers who try . . .

—Tom T. Hall

Sooner or later, and the sooner the better, you will learn the secret of good coaching: perspective.

Don't ruin your own pleasure or that of your players by taking soccer too seriously. There is nobody less appealing than a sullen loser, unless it's a gloating winner.

In your efforts to build a winner, there will be trying times. There will be losses, of all kinds.

There will be near-victories and there probably will be a walloping somewhere along the way. It is important how you deal with losing. It is especially difficult to preserve your competitive spirit and that of your team when the losses become consistent.

It's tough trying to win if you don't expect to succeed. One coach said, "We're getting to be the most graceful losers in the league; now I'd like a little practice in winning gracefully!"

In these times that try coaches' souls, you must never lose the respect of your players. You may drive them, but at the same time build them up . . . make them enjoy being driven. You won't need to tear them down, for the opponents will take care of that at game time. You must repair that damage and get them up for the next game.

It is difficult to analyze the quality called the will to win. You must convince your players that they won't be beaten until the last kick.

Charging Violently

Charging in The Back

Handling The Ball

Offside

Obstruction

Retire 10 Yards

Foul Throw

Advantage

Stop The Clock

Indirect Free Kick

Kicking

Tripping

Striking

Jumping

Pushing

Holding

REFEREE'S SIGNALS

Confidence is like electricity; complacency is a slow poison. Players who are winning often approach a game without the seriousness necessary. Sometimes a game they should have won will be out of reach before it dawns on them what has happened and it will be too late to pull themselves together.

Your tool for fighting off this overconfidence may be psychological. Caution them against "swell-headedness" and come down hard on the mistakes they are making even while winning. Scheduling a practice game against a more powerful team and letting them take their licks may be another answer. Benching one or more players who are causing a bad prevailing attitude may also do the trick.

There will be certain unavoidable pressures that will build up, but you can temper these barriers to a healthy attitude.

Winning is your goal, but not winning at all costs. Impress this upon your players. Their victories will be empty ones if gained by cheating or foul play. We're not talking only about youngsters, but older players, too. They feel pressures, too.

These pressures will not produce winners. You will be defeating your own purpose by teaching methods that will impose stress, for there will be a breaking point and you will lose not only games, but the players too.

If you have prepared your team properly, they will be ready to go on game day. They will know their jobs and they will be eager to get to work.

A pre-game pep talk can be an effective factor in your team's performance *and* attitude. One coach found that his halftime critique was getting more results than his pre-game talk. Before the game he had contented himself with reviewing strategy. His team invariably turned in a shoddy, non-aggressive half of soccer. At halftime, the coach would blow his gasket, tell them exactly what he thought of their performance and generally ruffle their digestion. A band of spirited tigers would return to the field and hustle their opponents off every ball. Needless to say, the coach got the drift and exercised the art of anger *before* future games.

Another champion pep talker outdid himself before a big game with a spirited address that ended with the traditional order to charge out and chew up the opponent. As the players flew to their positions, the team captain paused long enough to whisper to the assistant coach: "If we don't get off to a good start, you'd better send Coach Smith in. He's ready."

Many coaches find a more effective way to deal with the pre-game buildup is a quiet chat with each player while the teams are warming up. This will require knowing how to get the most out of each player. Some will respond to cajoling, others you must deal with more firmly.

Ron Newman, veteran coach of the Ft. Lauderdale Strikers and twice winner of the North American Soccer League's Coach of the Year award, says, "My key to successful coaching is to know the players well, both on and off the field. I try to keep the players happy and treat them with respect."

The player-coach relationship is more important than many coaches seem to know. It is essential that your players respect you and that will come about not only in your association with them, but in how you conduct yourself in relationships with others.

Rosemarie Graham, a well-respected lady referee in high school soccer, points out: "Coaches are great people—when they are coaching. But many seem to be closet referees. It's the coach who knows *almost* all the rules and is doing his best to let me know them who causes me the most consternation. I have attended more 'officiating clinics' while running a game than I have in a classroom. These 'clinics' can range from hissed suggestions while running the line in front of the coaches (probably the most dangerous spot on the field) to one brazen fellow who told me after a game that 'I belong in the kitchen.' It has been my experience that those coaches who spend their time coaching during games, not officiating, usually have better teams. Coaches, set the example for your players: follow the play, not the official."

These non-player relationships extend to your fellow coaches. Across the field, they, too, are trying to build a winning team. It will not go unnoticed when, after a tough loss, you meet your adversary in the middle of the field and congratulate him, maybe adding a word or two of praise for a few of the opposing players.

Happiness is the afterglow.

And, when you're in the driver's seat, don't pour it on. You will know instinctively when you have scored enough goals to win handily. Sometimes it's difficult. Maybe the subs you send in to keep the score down are so fired up, they're scoring, too.

Gus Pappas, coach at Chicago's Schurz High School was proud but embarrassed when his team ran up a record-setting 22-0 victory over a hapless opponent despite his efforts to stem his own team's tide.

"Everytime I turned around to apologize to the other coach," said Pappas, "we scored another goal!"

Occasionally, you will find yourself facing an opponent whose coach and players seem to be trying to annoy you and your team. Don't bother yourself about whether they are doing it deliberately or from habit. Keep your players from talking back to opposing players who try to needle them. Convince your players that it's important for them to play *their* game, not the opponent's. Team poise is as important as teamwork.

Your sideline behavior may have an effect on your players, too. Coaches of youth teams often run up and down the touch lines shouting instructions to the players because the youngsters are still learning. But yelling and screaming like a homicidal maniac will only confuse the players. If you have properly prepared your players for the game, they will need only an occasional reminder during actual play.

Make mental notes or write down areas of play that you feel need correcting and point them out at halftime or after the game. Keeping low key will instill confidence in your players and permit them to concentrate on their responsibilities.

Don't seek the impossible from your players. Be a leader, not a "boss."

The great soccer star Pele (left) with Coach Willy Roy.

Glossary

Beat—To outmaneuver an opponent by getting past him with the ball or getting into a position to receive a ball behind the defender.

Center—To pass the ball to the center of the field, usually in front of the goal.

Center circle—Circle drawn in the exact center of the field 10 yards in radius.

Center line—A straight line connecting the two side lines midway between the goal lines.

Charge—To use any part of the upper shoulder against an opponent to unbalance him.

Clear—To move ball away from the scoring area near the goal.

Corner kick—A direct free kick given the offensive team, taken within one yard of the corner of the field.

Cross—To pass the ball from a wide position on the field into the penalty area.

Defender—Primarily a defensive player who assists the goalkeeper in protecting the goal.

Direct free kick—A place kick which may result in a score when kicked into the goal.

Draw a defender—To induce an opponent to leave the player he is marking to mark the player with the ball.

Dribbling—To advance the ball by using the feet and touching the ball with short taps.

Drop ball—A means of putting the ball in play after temporary suspension.

Forward—An attacking player whose responsibility is to create and score goals.

Goal area—Portion of the field enclosed by lines drawn six yards into field from points six yards outside the goal posts.

Goalkeeper—Last line of defense. The only player who can use his hands within the field of play. He is restricted to using his hands only within the penalty area.

Goal kick—An indirect free kick taken by the defensive team within that half of the goal area nearest to where the ball crossed the goal line.

Goal line—The line marking the narrow end of the field.

Half-volley kick—To kick a ball the instant after it touches the ground.

Hands—Intentionally touching the ball with any part of the arms or hands.

Heading—To hit the ball with the head.

Holding—Obstructing a player's movement with hand or arm.

Indirect free kick—A place kick from which a score cannot be made until the ball is touched by another player.

Kickoff—An indirect free kick used as a means of starting each period of a game or restarting the game after a score.

Lead—To pass the ball ahead of the receiver.

Linkman—Another name for midfielder.

Mark—To defend; to remain so near an opponent that his efforts to play the ball would be hampered or nullified.

Midfielder—Player who plays in alignment between defenders and forwards.

Obstruct—To hamper movements of an opponent by remaining in the path he wishes to travel.

Overlap—Attacking play of defender going down the touchline past his winger.

Pass—To kick or head the ball to a teammate.

Penalty area—Portion of playing field bounded by lines drawn at right angles to the goal line 18 yards out from each goal post and 18 yards into playing field.

Penalty kick—A direct free kick taken from the penalty mark, 12 yards from goal line in center of goal posts.

Place kick—A kick at a non-moving ball placed on the ground.

Punt—To kick a ball as it is dropped from the hands.

Pitch—Another name for the field of play.

Save—The goalkeeper stopping an attempted goal by catching or deflecting the ball away from the goal.

Screen—Retaining possession and protecting the ball by keeping body between the ball and opponent.

Shootout—Tie-breaking procedure used in the North American Soccer League when teams are tied after playing two sudden death overtime periods. Teams take five alternating shootout attempts at opposing goalkeepers in one-on-one situation.

Sliding tackle—Attempting to take the ball away from an opponent by sliding on the ground.

Striker—Position of center forward.

Strong foot—The foot with which the player is most proficient.

Trap—To stop the ball near the feet.

Throw-in—Method of putting ball in play when it goes out of play over the side line.

Volley—To kick a ball that is in the air at any time other than the instant after it touches the ground.

Weak foot—The foot with which the player has the least skill.

Wing—Area of the field near the touchline.

Winger—Player nearest the sidelines on the forward line.

Index